Move, Mount, Shoot

MOVE MOUNT SHOOT

A Champion's Guide to Sporting Clays

John Bidwell with Robin Scott

The Crowood Press

First published in 1990 by
The Crowood Press Ltd
Ramsbury, Marlborough,
Wiltshire SN8 2HR

www.crowood.com

This impression 2008

British Library Catalogue in Publication Data

Bidwell, John
    Move, mount, shoot: a champions guide to sporting clays.
    1.Clay pigeon shooting
    I. Title II. Scott, Robin
    799.3'13

    ISBN 978 185223 3006

Acknowledgements

The authors are grateful for the help given to them by a
number of people and companies in the writing of this
book, among them the publishers of *Sporting Gun*,
Browning Sports, Winchester, artists Graham Gaches and
photographer Steve Moore. Last, but not least, thanks
must go to Sally and Hilary for their incredible patience.

Typeset by Acuté, Stroud, Glos
Printed and bound in Great Britain by
The Cromwell Press

Contents

Introduction

Sporting clays enjoys immense popularity – a happy state of affairs brought about, largely, by the fact that it is a game which can be played by people of all ages and both sexes; one which creates a lasting sense of achievement among its participants and, more important, one that allows individual skill to come to the fore in no small way.

Nowadays we live in an age when sophisticated machinery and office equipment have removed much of the need to demonstrate mental agility and manual dexterity so it is perhaps not surprising that people should turn to sports like clay pigeon shooting in ever greater numbers to create and satisfy personal challenges lost or stifled in workaday routine and sedentary leisure time.

Fishermen will probably disagree and say that there is no finer thrill than watching a salmon or trout rise to a fly of their own making but, to our minds, the sight of a clay pigeon being broken into lots of little pieces through individual skill is just as inwardly satisfying and rewarding. It is also infectious. Once a newcomer has smashed a few targets he can hardly wait to repeat the exercise. And very soon he will start to measure his enjoyment by the number of clays he hits against those he misses. This book will help him increase that enjoyment.

Library bookshelves already groan under the sheer weight of written material explaining how better scores can be made on Sporting grounds but this, as far as we are aware, is one of the first that looks in some detail at the use of a technique which allows the shooter to break targets with a method called Maintained Lead. As such we make no apology for adding to the tonnage and hope (nay, believe) that it will shed much needed light on the vexed question of hitting clay targets easily and consistently. The technique used is Move, Mount, Shoot.

It is crucially important to differentiate between the technique and the method because a great deal of confusion exists in the shooting world on how Maintained Lead can be used effectively on the many and varied targets encountered on a Sporting clays course.

Much of this confusion stems from the use of Maintained Lead on skeet ranges where the clays are thrown at constant speeds and along fixed paths. The speed and angles are so predictable, in fact, that a shooter knows he can swing the gun a predetermined distance in front of the clay and maintain that lead to break it every time. The Sporting shooter, of course, does not enjoy the same luxury. He has to recognise instantly what each target is doing and adjust the amount of lead (forward allowance) accordingly. If he tries to 'spot shoot' clays in the same way as he would skeet birds then he will be doomed to disappointment and inconsistency. Worse, he will convince himself that Maintained Lead is not for him and will doubtless return whence he came . . . to his usual style.

Yet prejudgement of lead is a common enough fault among would-be Maintained Lead shooters and one which is easy to avoid. The fault shows itself most often in a sportsman mounting his gun as soon as the target comes in view; he cannot wait to get the gun to the shoulder and, once there, deliberately picks a point in front of the target that looks right and maintains his chosen lead before squeezing the trigger. Invariably it is the wrong one.

In the pages which follow we will explain how Move, Mount, Shoot as a technique helps the sportsman overcome such distract-

7

ing mental imagery . . . by placing the emphasis instead on our unerring ability to steer the unmounted gun into position with natural eye-to-hand co-ordination. In other words, the barrels are brought to bear ahead of the target automatically with the lead being maintained throughout the mounting and shooting process.

It is an easy technique to master: what could be more natural than pointing ahead of a moving target? It is so natural that there is no need even to look at our extended arm and finger to check alignment. But, like any other shooting method you care to mention, the richest rewards will always go to those who apply themselves diligently to the job in hand and keep an open, enquiring mind to the set-backs that everybody suffers from time to time.

Before we take the gun from its slip, pocket a few cartridges and head for the shooting ground to put the technique through its paces we would like to point out that Move, Mount, Shoot is not a critique of other methods. Rather, it is a work intended to broaden the shooter's understanding of why he misses targets and how the technique can help overcome individual problems. It shares with other styles all the fundamental gun handling requirements needed for safe, enjoyable shooting so people who do decide to try it will find that it will not hamper their usual style should they decide to mix and match methods to suit the occasion.

We make no apology for the fact that *Move, Mount, Shoot* does not devote space to giving a detailed account of the rules under which English Sporting or International FITASC Sporting are conducted. These can be bought from the national shooting association for a small sum and are self-explanatory. They should certainly be acquired as a matter of course by anybody who takes part in competitions. Not only will the rule books increase understanding of how the two sports are run, but the knowledge thus gained will stand you in good stead should you ever need to question the decision of a referee.

Most referees worthy of the name know the rules inside out anyway but genuine mistakes do happen occasionally, and a polite, friendly query from the shooter at such times is usually all it takes to settle the matter. There is certainly no need – nor any excuse – for the regrettable antics of a minority who try to 'steal' birds by continually questioning decisions and putting the referee at each stand under pressure. Such people are tolerated but never made welcome at a Sporting ground. It is a pity they are too dense to realise it!

What we do apologise for is the lack of space which prevented us from exploring the overriding requirement for safe gun handling at all times. Weapons should be kept under lock and key when not in use, both to prevent theft and to stop children laying their playful hands on them. At the ground they should be carried broken or secured in a gunslip and only loaded when the sportsman is on the shooting station and ready to shoot. If there is a trap malfunction or the referee halts proceedings for whatever reason, the gun should be opened and unloaded immediately. If you are in a competition and the gun fails to fire, keep the barrels pointing down range and let the referee check things out. Never, never, turn round on the stand with a closed gun. It goes without saying that the bores should be checked for obstructions before cartridges are inserted into the chambers, and the gun should be checked again before the shooter steps off the stand to let the next man in.

It is because people take gun safety seriously that accidents, thankfully, are very rare indeed. Your enjoyment – and ours – rests on people wanting to keep this record intact and, in so doing, leave newspapers free to report the sobering fact that it is the motor car, not the shotgun, which kills on average sixteen people every day in Britain.

Throughout the book, for convenience, the shooter has been referred to as masculine. This approach does not mean to be sexist, but is just an expression of common usage.

1 Maintained Lead and its Place on the Shooting Scene.

Immeasurable amounts of paper and ink have been used over the years by people extolling the virtues of one shooting style or another. Ever since sportsmen started to shoot game birds on the wing in the eighteenth century, numerous authors and shooting instructors have been consuming the stuff in copious quantities so the totals must be fairly impressive by now. And we are still chopping down trees to feed the insatiable appetite of shotgunners wanting to improve their marksmanship!

Cynics might well argue that there is nothing new in shooting – that all the main styles propounded by instructors since the earliest days have common roots. To a point they would be right, of course: natural hand/eye co-ordination, proper footwork, smooth mounting of the gun, total concentration on the target and an unchecked swing are as true of the universally accepted Follow-Through system as they are of the controversial Churchill Method. And it is also true of the method that is the subject of this book – Maintained Lead.

So, if things have remained pretty much the same over two centuries, why isn't there a standard shooting style that everybody happily follows? And if good shooting does share common roots, why is it that one or more schools will argue until they drop that theirs is the better method and will always remain so?

To answer this, we must set aside, for a moment, the constituent parts of shooting and look instead at the real point at issue here: namely, the position of the gun barrels in relation to the target before, during and after the gun stock has been mounted into the shoulder. It is the key to the whole argument and the reason why so many trees have been felled over the years. Two words describe it:

FORWARD ALLOWANCE

Anybody who picks up a shotgun for the first time and fires off a number of cartridges very quickly comes to realise one thing – that to stand any chance of hitting a moving target the gun must be pointing ahead of it when the trigger is squeezed so that the shot intercepts it somewhere in its flight. How far in front (forward allowance) depends on a number of variables – target speed, its distance from the shooter, trajectory and a shooter's individual reaction time.

If we were all able to gauge distance and speed with pin-point accuracy and make an instantaneous mathematical decision on how long the shot pellets would take to reach each target, the problem would all but disappear: we would simply need to 'aim' the gun at the pre-selected mark and squeeze the trigger to be assured of intercepting the target every time. Unfortunately, human fallibility rules out this seemingly simple solution.

It would be wrong to say that the 'method' fails because the human brain is incapable of making an instant, and automatic, assess-

Good shooting relies on natural eye/hand co-ordination, an ability we develop at an early age. This playful youngster might be a year or two away from his first gun but he is already showing all the signs of being a highly competent performer!

The successful shot is the one who manages to get his gun the right distance ahead of a moving target more often than everybody else.

ment of what it thinks is 'about' right. It not only can, but does. That is why we are able to hit targets so consistently with the shooting methods available to us. Unfortunately, the system disintegrates because the speed at which the brain works not only varies from person to person, it changes from day to day (even hour to hour) depending on the individual shooter's physical and mental well-being at the time. This means that any fractional delay in reading the target or squeezing the trigger will result in the shot arriving too early at its destination or more probably, too late.

What we need, therefore, is a way of easing the burden on the grey matter in order to improve its chances of being able to make an instinctive and, usually, correct guess at the forward allowance needed to break the target. This has been neatly achieved, of course, by abandoning all thoughts of trying to shoot with a motionless gun, and instead, taking on board the idea that the brain can do its calculations much more effectively if the gun is moving with the target before the trigger is squeezed.

This gives us a definite advantage – our eyes are now better able to register all the information needed about the target and pass it instantly to the hands guiding the gun. Provided the chain of command is not broken by taking our eyes off the target, the shooter can rely on natural hand/eye co-ordination to adjust automatically for any quirk or characteristic in the target's flight. This ability is so accurate that, by the time the gun has been mounted to the shoulder, the barrels will be fairly accurately aligned with the target, leaving the shooter free to make any final adjustments to the forward allowance split seconds before firing.

How he makes this final adjustment is

11

*First lessons with a gun will leave a lasting impression. However, fresh
ideas can be taken on board and old ones discarded or modified if the will to
improve is strong.*

another matter altogether. However, it will
be largely dictated by the method he was
taught at the outset of his shooting career, as,
while he might dabble with modifications to
his usual style, the deep-seated basics will
always stay with him.

Experience plays a part in this because the
brain has the ability to store mental pictures
based on previous trial and error. In other
words, experienced performers can, to some
extent, control the urge to squeeze the trigger
until the relationship between the barrel and
the target is instinctively 'right'. Here instinct
has been moulded by previous success, but it
should not be forgotten that negative move-
ments are also filed away and will return as
regularly as the good points.

While it is right to allow these considerable

natural talents to influence our style of shooting, we must realise that, on their own, they
will not guarantee the level of consistent
accuracy a Sporting clay shooter is seeking.
To achieve this, instinct and ability must be
harnessed into a sequence of pre-planned
movement which can be controlled and used
to advantage shot after shot. In other words,
we need a 'method' and technique.

METHOD

As we have already seen, there are three
fairly distinct categories of 'method'. Each
has its own set of rules under which forward
allowance is achieved. It might help if we
look at each in turn.

Previous experience plays a large part in shooting. Success at breaking targets is a powerful aide-mémoire.

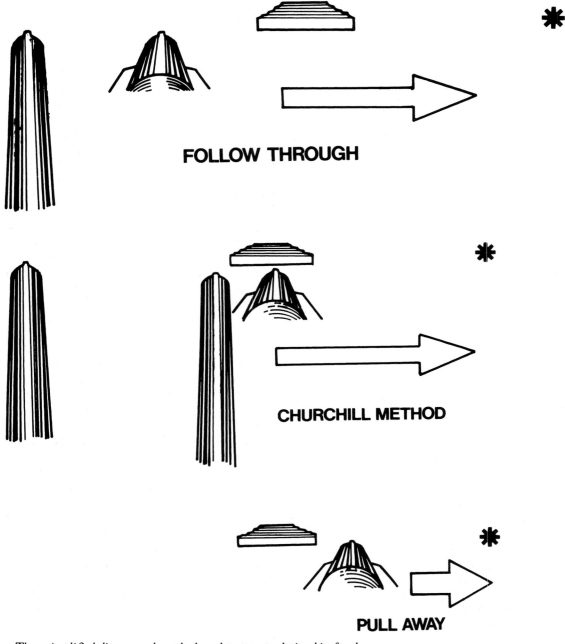

FOLLOW THROUGH

CHURCHILL METHOD

PULL AWAY

These simplified diagrams show the barrel-to-target relationship for the four main methods described here. The first two require that the gun is brought from behind and fired as the muzzles pass the clay pigeon. The Pull Away method represents something of a convenient half-way house but still requires that the shot is taken with an accelerating barrel.

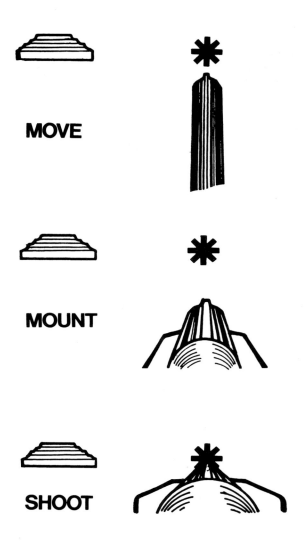

MOVE

MOUNT

SHOOT

Follow-Through

In the case of Follow-Through, the muzzles of the gun are held to the target's line of flight before the shooter calls for its release from the trap. As soon as he is able to see it clearly he starts moving the gun after it and lifts the stock to his face and shoulder at the same time. Provided he watches the target throughout the mounting process, the gun muzzles should end up sitting comfortably behind the target awaiting the next instruction – a conscious decision on his part to accelerate the gun through, and then past, the bird

before squeezing the trigger. In fact, it is this all-important spurt of speed that creates the forward allowance needed to break the clay.

While it is not the intention of this book to criticise any shooting style out of hand, it must be said that the need to accelerate a gun in this fashion does create a number of pitfalls for the unwary or inexperienced shooter. The critical element here is the speed at which the gun has to be moved after it is mounted to catch the target and pass it. Too fast, and there is a very real danger that the shot from the cartridge will miss in front; too slow and it will, in all probability, miss behind. But the drawbacks do not end there. If a shooter underestimates the speed of a target and is forced to compensate by rushing after it, he risks losing an element of control over the swing of his gun. This, for a style that relies on barrel speed for its success, is to say the least, rather appalling but greater complications are in store if the Follow-Through shooter also misreads a target's trajectory.

Imagine what will happen if he underestimates the initial speed of the clay target and fails to recognise that it is also starting to slow and drop below its earlier line of flight just as he sweeps passed it and squeezes the trigger: not only will the shot charge miss in front, but it will also go handsomely high as well!

Often a shooter will realise that he has overdone the lead and try to retrieve the situation by slowing (or stopping) the gun to let the clay catch up. Unfortunately, this ploy hardly ever succeeds. In fact, it is a fault which also tends to go hand-in-hand with lifting the head from the stock to get a better look at the target. And when this happens the shot will invariably miss high and behind.

So many things can go wrong when a shooter commits himself to pulling through a target that I would rarely recommend this as a method to a beginner trying to find reasons for why he misses. The only contribution it makes to his education is that to check the swing of the gun will result in the miss behind.

Speed of swing is everything to the Follow-Through shooter. If he gets this part of the equation wrong he is in deep trouble.

The Churchill Method

Speed and line of flight are also prime considerations when we come to look at the Churchill Method, a style that has generated much debate since London gunmaker Robert Churchill promoted it as an effective game-getter back in the 1920s. If Churchill ever acknowledged Follow-Through as a meaningful system then he kept very quiet about it, preferring instead to promote an unshakable conviction that his was a far neater way of getting the job done because it blended gun mount, swing and forward allowance into one package, rather than the other's two.

Churchill used his considerable skill with a gun to show that, by placing utter faith and total reliance on natural instinct and co-ordination, we could point at a moving object with unerring accuracy and rely on the mo-

mentum of the gun and our own reflexes to look after forward allowance.

He hammered home the need to devote all the attention to the target so that the shooter's gaze guided the muzzles of the gun: as long as the eyes remained riveted to the target and the body pivoted with it then the muzzles would come to rest on it, or very close behind it, when the butt hit the shoulder. All that was now left to do was to squeeze the trigger . . . the speed and momentum of the moving gun, plus a fractional delay between the brain giving the instruction to fire and the trigger finger carrying it out, being sufficient to deliver forward allowance in the right amount every time. If everything went according to plan, the shooter was left with the distinct impression that he had fired directly at the bird and had not given it any conscious amount of lead.

As with Follow-Through, Churchill's method has one or two points to commend it, not least the fact that, when performed correctly, it has an elegance and economy of movement that is a picture to behold. Unfortunately, 'instinct shooting' of such a pure nature has not endeared itself to Sporting clay shooters, one of the reasons being that participants do enjoy the luxury of knowing where the next target is coming from. More important, they also know where it is going and can afford to be a little more deliberate in the way they set themselves for the shot.

Another reason for the Churchill Method's low polling on the shooting range is that it places too much of an emphasis on the individual to cultivate a measured reaction to gun mount and the act of squeezing the trigger; this is no easy task when a shooter might be all fired up with anticipation at the start of the day and dog tired by the end of it. Timing, then, becomes a critical element with this shooting style.

Apparent and Actual Lead

Timing is also a word that covers a great imponderable to both methods, one which can cause untold confusion when we try to evaluate both methods: apparent and actual lead.

Apparent lead is a term used to describe the amount of forward allowance seen by the shooter between the target and his barrels at the very moment he pulls the trigger. It is less than the actual lead given because the barrel is travelling faster than the target as the shot leaves the barrels. 'Seen' is probably the wrong word to use here; 'aware' would be more appropriate because, regardless of the shooting style used, the act of imparting forward allowance is an instinctive operation relying totally on speed of swing.

However, the apparent lead given to a specific target will differ from shooter to shooter because, firstly, the speed of their accelerating barrels is unlikely to be exactly the same, and secondly, the reaction times to

passing the target and squeezing the trigger will be different. This means that on a clay that needs an actual lead of, say six feet, one Follow-Through shooter might admit to giving it a couple of feet while another gave it six inches.

This also goes some way to explaining why a 'Churchill' shooter will swear blind that he shot directly at the target to break it: his gun speed was such that no visible lead was apparent when he squeezed the trigger. The fact that his gun had travelled six feet ahead of the target between the moment the gun was directly on it and the time he decided to fire is, to such a stylist, neither here nor there. As far as he was concerned, he needed to shoot directly at the target to hit it.

Regardless of what a shooter does or does not see when he pulls the trigger, we should not forget that in both these methods the gun barrels must come from behind a target every time and finish up in front of it to be successful. Yet – as raw beginners have pointed out on my own shooting ground – if the object is to get the gun ahead of the target, why not start off ahead of it in the first place? Why not indeed!

Maintained Lead

Beginners are a very good example of how readily the concept of Maintained Lead can be absorbed and reproduced by somebody exercising an open mind. Some years ago I took a group of novices out to a tower stand at High Lodge, gave them a talk about safety and then let each of them try some dry gun mounting, mainly to check if they had any master eye problems. At no point were they told how to shoot the driven targets; the only instruction was that the gun had to move with the clay and that the shot had to be placed in front of it for them to stand any chance of breaking it. The result was remarkable, not because they each broke a very fair proportion of the targets, but because they slipped naturally into the pattern of a Maintained Lead shooter without the slightest

17

qualm. I never did get around to telling them about other shooting methods. They went home in blissful ignorance.

So what is Maintained Lead? Basically, it demands that the gun starts ahead of the clay when the target is first seen, stays in front of it during the entire gun mounting process and remains ahead when the gun is fired. It shares with the other two methods an absolute need to keep the eyes glued to the target and an equal need to keep the gun moving.

Its success as a consistent shooting method is, in some respects, a mirror image of the Churchill system in that it takes its strength from our ability to bring the gun into the line of flight by watching the target and moving our hands and body with it. But unlike the other, it does not demand that the gun moves faster than the bird to create forward allowance. Therefore it is not reliant on the changing fortunes of reaction times; nor (as in the case of Follow-Through) is it subject to the vagaries of barrel speed in overtaking the target. Instead, the gun takes its cue from the speed of the target and is directed into the required position by hand and eye co-ordination automatically.

People (especially shooting instructors!) have a very misleading notion of what Maintained Lead is, and how it is achieved. Most tend to think of it as a form of 'spot' shooting where the shooter picks a predetermined mark in front of the target, mounts the gun to it and temporarily tracks it before squeezing the trigger. This is simply not so. Pre-selecting a spot and watching that, not the target, is guaranteed to end in failure and send any doubting Thomas high-tailing it back to his usual method.

One gun writer has even gone on record as saying the method is one where the shooter mounts his gun ahead of the target and keeps it moving while he continually shifts his gaze from the gun to the target and back again. Only when the gap between the muzzles and bird looks right should the gun be fired. Bunkum!

Such people fail to grasp the fact that our hands and eyes are quite adept at bringing the muzzles of a moving gun into position ahead of a target without having to check their alignment with the clay before the trigger is squeezed. To take our eyes off the target in the way he suggests is guaranteed to check the swing as surely as a Follow-Through enthusiast will who, as we have already seen, pulls too far and too fast in front.

In subsequent chapters we will explain how a simple set of rules can be followed to allow these natural abilities of ours full rein on the many and varied targets to be found at a Sporting shoot. In the meantime we can look at the diagram opposite for a theoretical explanation of forward allowance. As you can see, the same amount of gun movement is needed on a 20-yard target as is required on one travelling at the same speed 40 yards away.

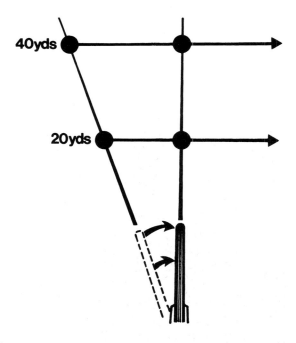

What isn't generally realised by novice shooters is that the gun movement needed to break a target at 20 yards with Maintained Lead will also break the bird at double the distance provided it travels the same speed and direction.

This simple equation applies whatever method of shooting is followed, but as the range increases so too does the difficulty in relating target speed to that of the gun. These 'aiming' difficulties are compounded in methods which rely on a shooter having to speed up his gun to get ahead. But Maintained Lead, by staying in front, does not suffer the same fate and, as such, has a number of inherent – and important – advantages over the others.

Now is an opportune time to say a word or two about a 'half-way house' style which curries favour with some Sporting clay shooters: the Pull-Away method.

The Pull-Away Method

If you stand behind somebody who shoots this way you can be fooled into thinking he is actually shooting Maintained Lead because the muzzles start ahead of the target and stay there when the gun has been mounted. But that is as far as the similarity goes. If you now watch the movement of the gun really closely you will see that once the stock meets the shoulder the barrels are speeded up in much the same way as Follow-Through to impart forward allowance.

The people most likely to drop neatly into the Pull-Away style are Follow-Throughers who find comfort in pulling away from a target while enjoying some, but not all, of the advantages of Maintained Lead.

No doubt it can be argued that so long as people using this bastardised style are happy with the results they get, they should be allowed to go their own sweet way because they are actually better off incorporating the best of both worlds. This, unfortunately, is not strictly so: their adoptive style is still subject in part to the changing fortunes of gun speed and reaction time.

Sceptics (and there are plenty in shooting!) will be wondering by now why, if Maintained Lead is so simple and effective, it is not more widely recognised in Britain.

Maintained Lead has shown itself to be a potent force on skeet ranges. The same method, albeit with a slightly different technique, offers the Sporting clays shooter the option of great consistency too.

The reason for this is historical. Those that have heard of it have a tendency to dismiss it as an American-bred system for shooting skeet, a discipline where all the targets follow predetermined, and rigid, speeds and lines of flight; a game where it is possible to mount the gun 'x' amount of inches or feet ahead of the target and maintain that lead until the shot has been fired. Others acknowledge its existence by admitting that they use it, or think they use it, on some types of Sporting targets.

But the real reason for its minority status here is that successive generations of shooting instructors have perpetuated the myth that consistent shooting can only be attained by bringing the gun from behind a target. When you realise that instructors normally only teach the method that they were taught then you start to appreciate the reasons why Follow-Through has become the most popular method in this country. It is a simple case of like begetting like and tough luck to anybody who asks for tuition based on Maintained Lead.

Thankfully, not all instructors are totally blinkered or blinded to the advantages which can accrue under the 'other' system. A point in case is a fellow instructor who rang to ask if I could book him in for two full days of instruction so that he could find out for himself what was involved and how the theory of keeping the barrels ahead of a target worked in practice. At the time, I was working on a series of instructional articles with *Sporting Gun* magazine and it was these that had brought a number of people to his door asking him for instruction. He showed commendable honesty in telling them he could not help. What the requests did do was create a resolve to find out more about the subject, hence his arrival on my doorstep.

Admittedly, he experienced a little difficulty adjusting to the technique but when the penny did finally drop there was no holding him. He could not believe how simple everything was, but when I asked him if he would now be incorporating it in his school's curriculum he said, 'Goodness no, it's more than my job's worth. If it was left to me then it would be taught as a matter of course but all the instructors that work with me have been told that school policy is to teach nothing else but Follow-Through, and Follow-Through it has got to be.'

I hesitate to name him and will only say that the establishment he belongs to has both an enviable and influential status in the shooting world.

The restriction, though, does not just apply to this one shooting school – it is, unfortunately, symptomatic of the ideology which permeates too many grounds in Britain today. Even the sport's governing body, The Clay Pigeon Shooting Association, has, in its own way, closed the door on Maintained Lead by giving official backing via its training committee to a style of shooting based on Follow-Through. I could be wrong, but I bet the instructors who guided the CPSA in its adoption of a training manual taught anything but Maintained Lead at their own ground.

In my view, it is a terrible shame that there are too few instructors able to give meaningful tuition in this method. What is even worse is the blatant way in which some tutors rubbish and ridicule it out of hand. Not only are they doing themselves a disservice by turning away custom, they are also holding back a great many people who are either trying to improve their scores or seeking an introduction to the richly varied world of Sporting clays.

2 Move, Mount, Shoot – Technique into Practice

Whoever coined the phrase 'good shooting is no accident' might well have been trying to promote safe gun handling but he could just as easily have been explaining how some people manage to achieve a level of excellence while others struggle to maintain even a modicum of mediocrity.

Good shooting certainly is not an accident, it rewards effort. But the encouraging thing is that better shooting is within everybody's reach provided they realise that there is more to marksmanship than 20/20 vision and perfect reflex action.

It is important to mention this now because some people are apt to lose heart rapidly in their own abilities if progress is not made quickly. Others, too, severely limit their progress by hiding their own shortcomings behind a smokescreen; they convince themselves that they will always be second rate because the people who do really well every weekend are 'naturals', people who can always be counted on to do well because they have been blessed with more than their share of natural talent at birth. Few would deny that excellent eyesight is worth having, but being able to spot a flea on a dog at ten paces does not necessarily mean that the holder of such talents will automatically become a terrific shot. Neither will instant reflex action guarantee a place in the front row.

Good shooting relies on much more than this. Above all, it demands an ability to channel the signals the brain receives from the target into a sequence of easy muscular responses which allow the body to pivot with it and which can be controlled and conditioned to advantage.

This means developing a technique and style that is both simple and uncluttered, because the fewer signals that need to be sent to the gun muzzles the better chance we have of programming a bodily response which can be relied upon. And nothing has happened in the last twenty years to make me change my mind about Maintained Lead being the easiest of all the styles to get to grips with. In fact, I will go even further and say that once a shooter has mastered the basics, the responses needed to break the target consistently will be carved on the mind in tablets of stone. The commandments will read: Move, Mount, Shoot.

These three simple, short instructions, create the chain of command that a Maintained Lead shooter needs to keep the muzzles of the gun in front of the target. No doubt this sounds complicated at the first time of reading but in practice it couldn't be easier – all it entails is making sure we get the position of our feet right!

This is because the feet dictate how far – and easily – our knees, hips and shoulders can rotate with the gun before the swing slows down and the muzzles are underneath the bird.

THE SHOOTING STANCE

The standard shooting stance is to stand with the heels of the feet about ten inches apart and the toes of the front foot pointing to an imaginary 1 o'clock position. Those on the other foot line up on 3 o'clock. The weight of the body is shifted slightly over the front foot.

Imagine now that you are going to shoot a

A comfortable ready stance for a right-handed shooter: feet about 10 inches apart with the toes on the leading (left) foot pointing towards the place where the clay target will be broken.

Better gun movement and control is achieved by pivoting with the body, not the arms. The position of the feet play a crucial part in dictating smooth, accurate swing throughout the Move, Mount, Shoot sequence.

Do not rush your shots just because other people are waiting to shoot. Make sure you are composed and properly positioned before calling for the target.

head-high crossing target passing from left to right and that the gun represents the arms of the clock. Mount the gun on the target and track it as far to the right as you can before any hint of stiffness is felt in the pivoting hip and knee of your leading leg. Now try swinging the gun the other way on a target moving from right to left.

Unless you are double-jointed you should find that the arc of unrestricted swing falls roughly between 11 o'clock to the left and 1 o'clock to the right, leaving the greatest point of unhindered movement directly in front at the 12 o'clock position. This is where you should always try to break the target.

Now put that leading foot at 11 o'clock and bring the other foot round to 1 o'clock before raising the gun on that left to right 'crosser'. The shift in body position might only be a few degrees but now try and shoot your imaginary target at 12 o'clock: just as you squeeze the trigger, those shoulders, arms, hips and knees of yours run out of movement and the swing of the gun stops. On the other hand, the right to left bird can be shot without any problem whatsoever. In other words, we must put ourselves into a position which has a bias on where the bird is

going rather than where it is coming from, otherwise the muzzles of the gun will be pulled off their line of flight and the shot will miss the mark.

The expression 'I missed because I misread the target' can often be heard on a shooting ground. If you ask whoever says it to explain what they mean, the reply will usually be that they did not realise the target was dropping (or rising) when they squeezed the trigger or that it was going faster (or slower) than they first imagined. Rarely will they say that their foot position was wrong, causing them to shoot under, over, in front or behind. Yet incorrect stance is responsible for more missed targets than all other faults put together.

The sobering part of this is that we know where the target is coming from and where it is going, so there is no real excuse for not adopting the right position to deal with it in the first place.

Ideally, we need to be able to look at a target and decide almost instantly where we should break it, and place our feet accordingly. However, there is no shame in standing for a few moments on the shooting position and running a mental picture of the target through our minds once or twice before shifting

23

Note how John has given himself extra swing on this left-to-right bird by turning his leading foot just past the point where he has taken the shot – a useful ploy when you are not totally sure about the speed of the target. In this instance he read it right first time.

those feet into place a few inches at a time. If you are not sure about the bird, take time out and call for it only when you are good and ready. Do not let the thought of people behind you waiting to shoot ruffle your composure and make you rush at the targets.

When you have decided where you want to break the target, take out a little bit of extra insurance by turning a degree or two further into the shot just in case it is travelling faster than you thought. Do not worry about any lack of speed on its part, or whether it is rising or falling, because with Maintained Lead the gun muzzles take their speed and direction directly from the target. The only reason for moving a little bit more in the direction of the shot is to create a greater arc of free movement should you need it.

As long as you appreciate why the feet need to be placed properly to tackle different targets, you will be surprised at how quickly you start adopting the right stance for the target without any real conscious thought or effort. This is as it should be and runs in parallel with any other sport where the participants are faced with a moving ball or object. Cricketers and tennis players spring straight to mind as people who use (and trust) their natural co-ordination to strike the target consistently. They keep their eyes on the ball and never once look down to check that it is in line with the bat or racket. They do not even have to check that their foot position is right to pull off the cover drive or top-spin lob that suddenly presents itself as they move into the shot; they simply make their minds up that that is the shot they want to play, keep a close eye on the ball and get on with it – their feet drop into the right position automatically.

CONCENTRATING ON THE TARGET

The same applies when you come to shoot Maintained Lead. Keep your eye on the target, Move the gun, Mount and Shoot in one

easy movement. Never, never be tempted to let your eyes drift from the target to check its relationship with the gun barrel because this will simply result in the swing of the gun being checked momentarily and the shot being sent harmlessly behind the target. It can also lead to the shooter committing another cardinal sin: lifting his head from the stock to get a better look at the target. The shot will now pass harmlessly over the top of the clay as well as missing it behind. At least we do not suffer the same consequences as a cricket batsman who takes his eye off the ball. Rather than a missed clay that sails harmlessly on, he is faced with a rocketing ball that can hit him in the sort of places which make him wish he had taken up clay shooting after all . . .

By checking the position of the barrels, a shooter loses a large measure of the controlled response that is set in motion by his first, clear, sight of the clay. Such a lapse in concentration hampers our first, and usually correct, instincts about the target because valuable moments are lost by the eyes focusing on the clay, then the gun and, back to the target. Even a slow-moving clay pigeon will have covered quite a bit of ground while the eye is flickering back and forth as we try to measure out the right amount of forward allowance. Unfortunately, it hardly ever works because the interruption caused by a shooter switching his attention from one to the other automatically slows the swing of the gun.

This is not to say that a shooter will be totally oblivious to the rib of the gun when it is being mounted into the shoulder. Even when he is concentrating hard on the target, a sportsman will almost always be aware of the rib creating a faint, indistinct line in his peripheral vision. With experience, the shooter can learn to use this fleeting image to double-check the lead he is giving a target just before he pulls the trigger. But the secret is to fight any urge to shift that focus from the target to the gun. Instead, we must learn to live with it and disregard it just as we would the emblem on the bonnet of a car and keep watching, instead, the space beyond.

Right: *the shooter's eyes are focused on the target and the rib of the gun is blurred.*

Wrong: *the eyes have transferred to the barrel causing the swing of the gun to slow. The clay has closed the gap and the shot will miss behind.*

POINTING THE GUN

One area of the Move, Mount, Shoot instruction which always draws a question or two from people trying the method is: 'Where do I point the gun before calling for the target?'

This is easily answered in those methods where the gun comes from behind the target: you simply place the gun muzzles on the line of flight, pivot back towards the trap house with the gun and then, when the target appears, move the gun smoothly after it. As we have seen already, the gun will be pointing just behind (or on) the target when the butt reaches the shoulder, leaving the shooter no option but to accelerate through and in front of it before the trigger is squeezed.

With Maintained Lead the gun is not taken as far back to the trap. The last thing we want is for the target to pass the muzzles of the gun, so the point we need to address is the one which allows us to see the target clearly and react to it before it can close the gap. If the target should overtake the barrel before the shooter responds to it and starts Moving the gun the hold position is too close to the trap. Equally, we must not start too far in front either because this will merely encourage the shooter to Move too soon and, in all probability, lead to the gun being Mounted early. Usually this will result in the clay being missed in front but there is also a fair chance that, to make amends, the gun will be slowed or stopped altogether to give the target a chance to catch up. The upshot of such erratic behaviour is to bring about an emphatic miss behind.

A pretty accurate rule-of-thumb guide to getting this important aspect of Maintained Lead right is to determine where you will get your first clear view of the target and also where you can shoot it comfortably. This last point (we call it the sweet spot) will dictate the position of the feet. What you must now do is look back to the target's entry point and let the gun barrels assume a position midway between the two.

Wherever possible, always try to 'pivot'

back to this predetermined gun hold position by rotating those hips and shoulders. Don't get lazy! Never lift the gun into the ready position through arm movement alone because all this will create is an inhibited posture where the gun lies across the chest and closes down the shoulder pocket, leaving the gun butt little option but to come to rest on the upper arm or shoulder socket when the gun is mounted. The big disadvantage here is that by bringing the arms into play without the trunk a shooter loses an important element of control and direction when the gun starts to move. In addition to this, the head is liable to move in a manner that makes consistent mounting a near impossibility. How? Remember that shotguns, unlike rifles, do not have convenient backsights to help us place an accurate shot. This function, instead, is fulfilled by our master eye which must assume the same position above the stock and gun rib each time the stock is mounted. This being so, it follows that the gun stock must be brought to the same place in the face and shoulder for every shot. If it isn't our accuracy will suffer, just as a rifleman's steady aim would go to pieces were his backsight to keep slipping between rounds.

Pivoting with the shot has a number of advantages. Firstly it keeps the shoulder pocket nicely open and in line with the gun butt, allowing it to slide sweetly into place; secondly, the rotating shoulders ensure that the head and eyes not only move at the same speed as the body and moving gun but they also stay level and come to rest in the right place on the stock for shot after shot accuracy.

Other factors come into play here too, particularly the fit of the gun, but this subject is dealt with in Chapter 12. For the time being, we assume that the reader is right-handed and using a gun which, when mounted with both eyes open, leaves the comb resting comfortably in the cheek while the right eye takes up a position directly in line, and slightly over, the rib on the top of the gun. All that needs to be said here about gun fit is that the shooter should avoid using a

Wrong: *John has set himself to take a low left–right crosser in a position occupied by the camera lens. His foot position is right, but he has used his arms to lift the gun across his chest, closing down the shoulder pocket and leaving his head too erect in the process. The gun mount is going to be erratic and the swing will lack control.*

28

Right: *John has brought the gun to bear on the hold point by 'breaking' the right knee and turning from the waist. This in turn allows him to rotate his chest, shoulders and head. Note how the shoulder is right behind the line of the stock. His body is now in full control of the swing and mount.*

weapon which encourages him to adopt an unnatural head down, or head up, position and so arrive at the rib-to-eye relationship we have just been talking about. If a sportsman must resort to some sort of unfortunate contortion to get his eye into position then he is severely hampering the co-ordinated movement that is paramount to good shooting. What we must strive to achieve is a smooth and regular gun mount and swing; one that is produced, directed and edited by the eye and body. Anybody who contrives a style is simply storing up problems for the future, problems which will surely surface when they are under pressure, tired or excitable.

GUN POSITION IN RELATION TO THE LINE OF FLIGHT

Before closing this chapter there is just one more point that needs to be borne in mind by the Maintained Lead shooter: gun position in relation to the line of flight.

Most exponents of Follow-Through prefer to adopt a gun hold position that leaves the muzzles directly on the target's line of flight so that when the gun is mounted it is already moving in the same plane as the clay and needs only to be swept through and in front to bring about a successful shot. Followers of this method will happily point out that the only sure way of determining a target's speed and line of flight is to bring the gun from behind. This argument, though, belittles the ability of the eye and brain to work out what is happening without the help of a 'yardstick' in this case, the gun. Our eyes can manage quite well on their own.

Follow-Through is fine so long as the shooter (especially on fast targets) has managed to work out the bird's line of flight before he calls for it. This is because he might find himself with precious little time to compensate for a hold that is too high or too low once the clay has been released and gone past the barrel.

There is another point to bear in mind as well: regardless of shooting style used, there are times when the gun barrel obscures the view of the target just before the shot is fired. All a shooter can do is keep swinging and fight any and every temptation to slow down or lift the head to re-establish visual contact.

Maintained Lead, however, does minimise the problem because rather than addressing the target's line of flight, the gun muzzles are kept slightly below its path – especially on any clay that has lateral direction to it, as in the case of a crosser. By keeping the muzzles just underneath we can keep the bird in much clearer view and let our eyes and hands direct the gun into position.

Do not be tempted to hang on to the shot once the stock has bedded itself firmly into the cheek and shoulder. Trust in your hands and eyes, squeeze the trigger and keep the gun moving at the same speed.

If you are still not convinced that the human eye can 'read' a target unaided, it might be as well to return to our cricketer for a moment: he has finished his batting stint and is now out in the covers as a fielder. One of the batsmen gets his shoulder behind a wayward ball and hits it, hard, in the direction of our man. Notice that he keeps his eye on the ball, takes three or four quick paces to get into position, extends his arm out in front at the last moment and takes a neat catch just over his right shoulder. Notice too that he did not wait until the ball had passed him before moving his hand and arm. Neither did he stand like a traffic policeman with his arm raised waiting for the ball to arrive. Of course he didn't! He did what all of us are capable of doing – watching the ball and allowing our eyes and brains to tell us when to move and steer our hands into position.

The same guidance system comes into play in shooting if only we would let it. Substitute a clay for the ball, put a gun in his hands and watch him bring the muzzles up, and into, the path of the bird every time. Simple!

3 Choosing a Gun

Take a look in any well-stocked gunshop and you will find a staggering array of shotguns on show: short-barrelled skeet guns, long-barrelled trap guns, side-by-side game guns, semi-automatics, pump guns, guns with detachable chokes, guns with interchangeable stocks, stocks with high combs, low combs, guns for wildfowling and guns for pigeon shooting. And that's before you move on to the racks holding the myriad guns purpose-built for Sporting clays!

What is really mind-boggling is that all of them – and a few more besides – can be pressed into service. It would be way off the mark to say that guns which do not have the magic word 'Sporter' stamped somewhere on their furniture cannot be used for this particular shooting game. That, in many respects, is one of the beauties of the sport. Take a look around any shooting ground and you will be sure of finding somebody turning theory on its head by hitting targets with a gun that the 'purist' would regard with contempt.

The choice of guns for Sporting clays is staggering and likely to bewilder the first-time buyer. But with a little care, guidance and advice a suitable gun will be found.

I have seen enough game shooters with side-by-sides in my time, along with wild-fowlers clomping along with clumsy pump guns, to know that it is the man, not the gun, that determines how many clays end up broken.

Whenever I do see somebody shooting well with the 'wrong' gun, though, I cannot help but wonder just how much better they would fare were they to use one that was built for the job. This is because a more suitable weapon makes life so very much easier. It smooths out the bumps and wrinkles that come during the course of a practice session or competition and works with, rather than against, the shooter when the pressure to shoot well is really on.

By all means stick with that lightweight game gun or ponderous 32-inch wildfowling weapon if you only see Sporting targets as convenient closed season practice for the real thing or as a spot of light relief after a hard week at work. But if you really want to shoot well and wring every last bit of enjoyment out of this fascinating sport in its own right, get an Over and Under that (if not exactly built for the job in hand) will help and not hinder your progress.

Gun buffs are fond of comparing the handling characteristics of O/Us against those of conventional guns where the barrels are arranged alongside one another. They seem to set great store on the latter's supposed better pointability and easier get up and go qualities which stem mainly from their lighter weight.

These admirable traits are all very well in the game field where a gun might have to be carried long distances between shots. On a shooting ground the O/U comes into its own in no small measure.

Chief consideration now is for a gun that can fire 100 or more cartridges in a relatively short space of time without unduly punishing the user with recoil. The comparatively bulky fore-end and pistol grip stock of the mass-produced O/U might look clumsy compared to the snake-like lines of the other, but the better control they give the shooter in holding down muzzle flip and riding out recoil is well worth having.

Unfortunately, this still does not answer the question: which one is best for Sporting?

Like it or not, the main deciding factor is price and how much shooting you want to do. There is little sense in spending £2,000 if you only expect to shoot 200 cartridges a year. Equally, a £200 gun is unlikely to stand up to the punishment very well if it is fed a diet of 15,000 shells or more in the same period. Repeated recoil on such a grand scale will test its mettle in more ways than one and find weaknesses you were unaware of. This is not to say that the same gun will not give sterling service over many years if it is used lightly and properly cared for.

If this is making out a case for a middle-of-the-road model, then so be it. Thousands of sportsmen who settled for a new gun costing £600 to £1,500 at 1989 prices will have had few causes to grumble and will probably still be shooting it on a regular basis well into the next century. Keeping them company will

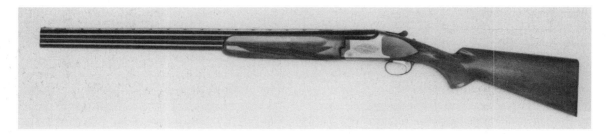

A sensible, middle-of-the-road Sporter like this Miroku 3800 is a long-lasting choice for many sportsmen.

be countless owners of serviceable second-, third- and fourth-hand weapons, guns made by highly reputable makers but selling for little more than the amount you might have to pay for a good middle-range model.

The choice can be truly staggering. But finding the right gun need not be a nightmare. Follow a few simple rules, talk to other sportsmen, always try before you buy and you will find that the process can actually lead to a lot of fun . . . much the same, in fact, as finding the right spouse!

Take plenty of time before making your mind up. Nobody wants to spend the happiest days of their life being kicked from pillar to post or forever having to patch up and put up because the object of their desires proves temperamental and unreliable.

Fashion, to some extent, plays a part in what Sporting clay shooters find acceptable. This is especially true of barrel length and choke systems. Until a few years ago competitive clay shooters tended to use 28-inch and 30-inch guns as a matter of course but then somebody hit a winning streak with shorter barrels and decided that these were the things to have. But the trend was short lived and the pendulum quickly swung from 25- and 26-inch guns back to 28 and 30 inches. Some champions are even using 32-inch guns now, but unless you know exactly what you want in a Sporting shotgun it is best to steer well clear and play safe.

If you are undecided about which barrel length suits you best, the only way to find out is to borrow guns from friends, try each and settle on the one you feel most comfortable with.

When it comes a length of gun barrel always let your physical size and strength determine the choice, never the targets. Long barrels might help on long-range birds but what about all those thrown fast and close? Pick a length that you can control.

There will always be exceptions to the rule but a reasonable guide is to let your physical size and strength determine the choice. Long-barrelled guns in the hands of a slightly built shooter can prove to be rather unwieldy to say the least. Similarly, short whippy barrels are unlikely to do a muscular six-footer any favours either.

Do not fall into the trap of thinking that close-range, fast targets need short barrels to deal with them effectively, or that long barrels give extra pointability on far-away targets. We have already seen that Maintained Lead works best when eyes, hands and body steer the gun into the path of the target so we should always try to settle for a barrel length that lets us do this easily without strain or any loss of control, which is determined mainly by a shooter's physical strength and size.

The balance of a gun should also be taken into account here because it is a quality which has a major bearing on how well the shooter can control the barrels during the Move and Mount sequence. However, balance should never be confused with a gun's overall weight since it does not necessarily follow that a heavy gun is also badly balanced. Wherever possible, of course, stay away from excessive weight because while it might soak up uncomfortable recoil it will cause fatigue during a long shooting day. Tired muscles play havoc with gun mounting, and once this happens accuracy and enjoyment go downhill at an ever increasing rate.

Beware, too, the lightweight gun which might move neatly and crisply to the shoulder: its lack of momentum can easily contribute to an erratic swing and will doubtless allow recoil to punish the user unnecessarily.

Most shooters accept that a well-balanced gun is one which puts the weight between the two hands holding it. A common enough test to see how a gun measures up is to rest the gun carefully on an outstretched index finger and keep adjusting its position until the see-sawing motion between muzzles and stock ceases. If it is agreed that the weight of the gun should rest between the hands, this balance point should finish up on, or near, the barrel to action hinge pin.

There is, however, a tendency with some guns to balance a few inches forward of this. Those that do might well earn themselves the tag of being 'muzzle heavy' but they have been made this way for a purpose; the makers have built in swingability so that people who come from behind a target will find that the increased momentum of the gun reduces the risk of slowing, or stopping, the gun just as they pull the trigger.

I would hesitate to recommend a gun displaying this sort of characteristic to anybody using Maintained Lead because in extreme cases the forward weight can affect the ease with which a Maintained Leader must respond to the movement of the target.

It is not necessary, though, to reject a gun exhibiting a tendency toward muzzle heaviness if, in every other respect, it appeals to – and suits – the shooter. Imbalance at the front end is quite easily remedied by securing slivers of lead in the hollow gun stock to bring the balance point rearward. Similarly, if the gun displays muzzle lightness, wood can be removed from the stock, but this job is best left to a skilled gunsmith who knows exactly what to do.

Bear in mind as well that if the stock is lengthened, or shortened, by an appreciable amount, the gun's balance can be affected. This is especially so if a shooter removes wood from the stock of a long-barrelled gun or adds a heavy extension pad to the butt of a gun with short, light barrels.

The loss, or addition, of two or three ounces in weight at the butt end might not seem a lot at the time but it can make a great difference to the way the gun handles and determine how well, and easily, you shoot.

Another feature of O/U guns that is worth looking at briefly is the rib which runs from the standing breech to the muzzle end of the barrel. Sporting shooters have some funny notions about what this feature does and does not do. In one breath they will happily tell anybody who cares to listen that when they hit targets they are never aware of the rib or barrels encroaching on their vision; all they do is watch the clay and throw the gun to their shoulder before pulling the trigger. Yet in the next breath they are just as liable to hold forth about how their rib's marvellous pointability has improved their shooting in no small measure!

The size and shape of rib on an O/U can – and does – influence the gun's apparent 'pointability', but this is not its sole, nor primary, function. Unlike a side-by-side shotgun, an O/U does not need a top rib to hold the two barrels together and, as such, is not crucial to its functioning.

Instead, the slotted metal strip fitted to the top barrel has been put there to dissipate and disperse the heat generated by hot gases from the cartridge. Properly shaped and designed ventilated ribs push heat haze away from the top of the gun so that the shooter's

Width of gun rib is a very personal thing. Choose the one which you find least distracting when the gun has been mounted.

master-eye view of the target is not impaired when the gun has been mounted. Similarly, the top surface of each rib is given a matt finish and file cut to reduce the risk of sunshine or strong light creating a glare which could prove equally distracting.

Very few shooters are not aware of the rib when they mount the gun and pull the trigger. Some notice it more than others but it will be there all the same, usually as an indistinct line. In fact, it should never appear to be anything other than a hazy intrusion on a shooter's field of vision because once you start noticing it there comes a temptation to switch the focus from the clay to the gun and stop the swing in the process. This does not mean that a sportsman should not be aware of the rib's position when the stock is mounted.

A fleeting sight picture of the correct lead split seconds before the shot is fired can often be of great help, even to a Maintained Lead shooter who will normally bring the gun muzzles to the right position ahead of the clay anyway. It does no harm to file away 'sight pictures' like this and use them from time to time as an instinctive double check that the lead you are giving a difficult target is correct. The secret is to make sure it remains a subconscious fail-safe and does not become a conscious action.

The actual width of the rib is, again, very much a matter of personal preference. The secret is to find one which does not intrude on your vision too starkly. For instance, I find wide ribs far too distracting and, given the choice, will always pick a gun with the narrowest rib possible as this lets me concentrate on the target far better. This, of course, is not to say that the same rib would suit everybody else.

It is not within the scope of this book to delve too deeply into the complex, and fascinating world of chokes and choke performance. There are plenty of good books on the subject and I strongly recommend that you track one down and read up on it. You will find it time well spent.

The question most often asked though by

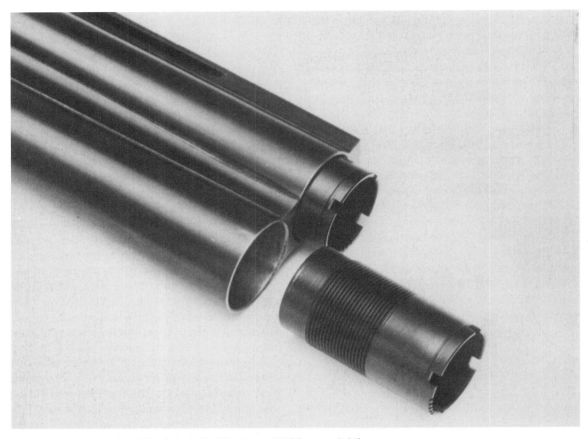

Screw-in chokes like these Winchokes off a Winchester 6500 have made life so much easier for the Sporting shooter. He no longer needs two or three guns with different choke in the barrels to cope with all eventualities. However, they do need cleaning after each outing to ensure that they do not stick in the barrel.

people buying a new, or second, gun is whether they should choose one with interchangeable screw-in chokes or settle, instead, for the more traditional 'fixed choke' configuration. Fixed choke is in inverted commas because at one time a gun would be supplied as a matter of course with varying degrees of choke in one or both barrels. Ever since guns with screw-in chokes became massively popular it has become necessary to refer to the others as being non-changeable, hence the term 'fixed choke'.

There is no doubt that the multichoke gun has revolutionised English Sporting. No longer is it necessary to carry two (sometimes three) guns with different degrees of choke in the barrels around a Sporting layout to cope with all eventualities. A sportsman now need only cart along one gun with a set of six choke tubes to cover any and every possibility. Within minutes he can remove the heavy choke needed on the last stand's long crossers and replace them with more open borings to handle the next batch which might be close-driven birds. The permutations are well nigh endless.

Interestingly, a great many sportsmen soon tire of the novelty and eventually end up

It takes time to get to know a gun. Anybody who continually chops and changes will not be doing himself any favours.

Few serious Sporting shooters use a side-by-side gun; they prefer the pointing characteristics of the single rib O/U and appreciate its greater control under repeated recoil. Some big championships incorporate a special side-by-side class but even experienced men weigh in with scores well below those posted by O/U users.

shooting the gun with one set of chokes installed almost permanently because they cannot be bothered to change them at every stand. Often these will be quite open borings as well. It is not unusual to find people happily using ¼ and ½ choke or even ¼ and ¼ on everything that's thrown their way, including distant midi clays, where once they would have settled for nothing less than ¾ and full choke.

In some respects, World Sporting Champion A.J. Smith helped to set the ball rolling for very open borings by shooting some incredibly long birds with nothing more than ¼ and ¼ choke to win his title in 1987. What he did not say at the time was that he had no choice in the combination because his screw-in chokes had welded themselves into the barrels!

Even though the case for permanent chokes has been well made it is unlikely that the multichoke gun will ever lose its popularity because the choice it gives is an enduring selling point. Whether clay shooters will ever make full use of the options available to them is not important. What is important is that the system has encouraged more and more people to shoot with just one gun.

Anybody who wants to develop to their full potential can only do so by getting used to the way their gun handles. By using one gun all the time a shooter is able to hone his reflexes in a way that the man who switches weapons from one outing to the next never will. Any variation in the weight, balance (even strength of trigger pulls) from one gun to the other will affect the shooter's response to the target and so prove detrimental to his performance.

A cupboard full of guns might be a source of satisfaction to the shooting enthusiast but they will not make him a better shot. Find a gun you like and stick with it.

4 Cartridges

Good shooting is all about putting the gun in the right place at the right time ahead of the target. But it is the cartridge that breaks the clay, not the man behind the stock.

Nowadays cartridge loading and the components used are so consistently accurate that rare indeed are misfires. Even rarer are cart-wheeled or balled patterns of yesteryear, by-products of inferior wadding materials which either unsettled the column of shot as it left the barrel or which failed to create an effective seal in the bore, allowing hot powder gases to leak past and weld the pellets into useless clumps.

The fashion now is for one-piece plastic cup wads. These not only protect the relatively soft lead pellets from the fierce heat propelling them up the barrel but also prevent them from being scrubbed out of shape against the wall of the barrel. Such aberrations as used

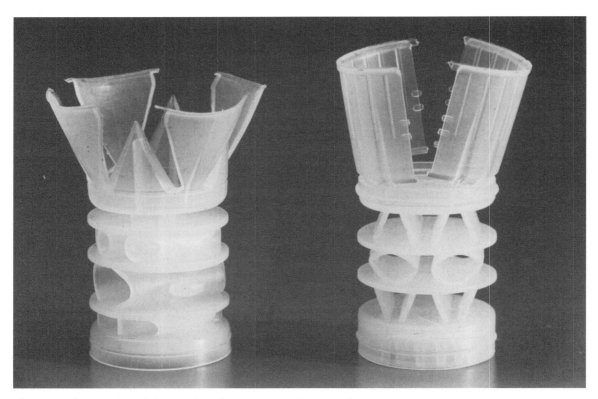

One-piece plastic wads and shot cups have become commonplace in modern ammunition. These were taken from a skeet cartridge (left) and a trap shell. The leaves surrounding the shot charge protect it as it passes through the barrel but peel open after, leaving the gun to let the pellets carry on alone.

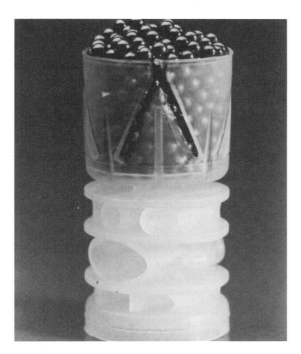

The series of skirts supporting the shot cup are designed to cushion the shot from the forces of ignition and also produce a gas-tight seal in the bore of the gun.

to occur are now so rare that they can be discounted: so much so that it is worth repeating here the oft-quoted maxim that if we were ten per cent as consistent as the worst cartridges on the market we would hardly ever miss another target!

That we do enjoy such evenness in performance can be attributed to the work of the loader and the ability of modern computer-controlled machinery to churn out technically correct cartridges by the thousand every hour. Each brightly coloured case that comes off the conveyor belt and drops into the cartons we buy in the gunshop is, in reality, a mass-produced work of art. Yet shooters rarely stop to give the loader's skill a second thought as they feed another fresh round into the chamber, close the gun and squeeze the trigger again and again . . . and again. All they demand is that when the gun is pointing in the right direction the clay breaks into lots of satisfying little pieces, the more pieces the better. And all the loader demands by way of recognition and job satisfaction is repeat orders.

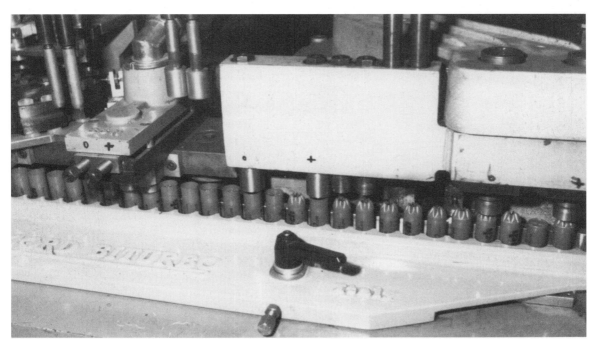

Cartridge loading

This is a fairly simple arrangement of supply and demand but cartridge loaders know only too well that competition to produce an effective load at a price which finds favour with the shooter runs at an incredibly high level, and any brand that does not come up to scratch on one – or both – counts is liable to get by-passed pretty smartly. This is good from the shooter's point of view because it ensures that the sport remains a buyer's market: prices stay within reach, yet allow (despite what some manufacturers might say!) sufficient profitability to fund extra research and development into making ammunition even more effective and fun to use.

While shooters, in the main, do not really care about the technical niceties of pellet

Few shooters engross themselves in the technical niceties of cartridge loading. All they want to know is that their chosen brand will do everything asked of it . . . and that it remains affordable.

antimony levels, wad types, powders and primer heats, they do take an interest in how the cartridge breaks targets through their own gun and how it feels on the shoulder. Most have an interest in how fast the pellets cover the distance between the muzzle of the gun and the target itself.

PELLET SPEED

While ultra-fast pellet speed (velocity) is something which appeals to most users, there are limits beyond which the manufacturer dare not pass, and which the customer would not thank him for if he did. For a start, increasing the speed usually means increasing the powder load to drive it with extra force up the barrel or choosing one which burns more violently. Unfortunately, both options can raise the pressures inside the barrel to unacceptable levels, push up the amount of recoil and worse – reduce the very quality and evenness of pattern which shooters hold as sacrosanct.

Indeed, the constraints placed on the loader by the laws of physics (not to mention the proof house where each new load has to be tested before it can go on sale) are such that, if any shooter were carefully to measure each popular competition cartridge on an accurate chronograph, it is doubtful whether he would find more than 150 feet per second velocity separating the fastest from the 'slowest'. Mathematicians will tell you that a typically 'slow' shell turning in at 1050 f.p.s. and another at 1200 f.p.s. make little practical difference to the amount of forward allowance needed to break a target. If there is an advantage it will be measured in meagre inches rather than feet.

Yet this does not explain why some cartridges give the shooter the distinct impression that one cartridge seems to get to the target faster than another with fairly similar velocity values. In this respect, some people will swear blind that there is a noticeable difference. However, the sensation more usually can be traced to the rate at which the powder reaches peak pressure after ignition and, especially, the type of recoil it generates and feeds into the gun stock and the shoulder stopping its rearward travel. While a shooter might be left with little sensation of recoil from a fast-burning powder that reaches peak efficiency in the twinkling of an eye, he is more likely to register the ponderous, deliberate push from one that burns more steadily and reaches operating pressure in a much more progressive manner.

RECOIL

Most shooters are agreed that there is nothing worse than a cartridge which produces uncomfortable levels of recoil. Not only is the sensation physically uncomfortable (even painful if poor gun mounting leads to bruising)

but in the course of a long day excessive inertia of this kind tires the muscles and dulls a sportsman's reactions and powers of concentration. In its worst form, the shooter will respond to growing tiredness by dreading the thought of having to pull the trigger again, but even before this stage is reached his accuracy and consistency will be on a downward spiral.

Of course, this subject of recoil will always be one of degree; what might be very acceptable to one shooter could be intolerable for somebody who is recoil sensitive or uses a lighter gun than the other man. While there is great fun to be had out of trying different cartridge brands to see if they do have any advantages over your usual variety, such journeyings should be tempered with care and understanding. Certainly, a decision to buy several thousand on the strength of a 25-bird practice session should be avoided

The hardest-hitting cartridge in the world will be worth naught if a shooter finds that it rattles his fillings and causes him to flinch. Each will settle on a shell he can cope with.

43

wherever possible until you have had time to put them to a more meaningful test and compared the results carefully against the averages you normally record. After all, where is the sense in losing targets that would usually be broken because cumulative tiredness has taken an insidious hold?

In the main, people find that they can change from one shell to another without encountering such problems but, regardless of how well we are able to adapt, there are advantages in finding a small selection that cover all eventualities and sticking with them. Not only will a shooter get used to the feel of the recoil and so subconsciously discount its presence but the confidence in the way the cartridge breaks the target will also let him devote full concentration to where it is most needed – on the target.

In some respects, this conditioning of our senses and shoulder to memorise the 'finger-print' of a cartridge is little different to that of training our muscles and reactions to the weight and balance of the gun. In time, both become part and parcel of a technique which benefits from having no outside distractions nor inner interferences, and, as such, our standard of shooting can only benefit.

PATTERN QUALITY

Occasionally letters crop up in the shooting magazines where a sportsman criticises his, hitherto, reliable cartridge for suddenly behaving differently. Either it is recoiling more than usual or going off with a noticeably lower report. This begs the question: are these just poor batches which have got passed quality control in the factory or has the manufacturer changed the components for some reason? When the enquiry is pursued it normally transpires that the cartridges in question have been loaded with single – as opposed to double – based powders and stored in either abnormally warm or cold conditions where the temperature change has affected the powder's rate of burn. It has

to be said that such differences that do occur are minor and do not pose a danger to the gun or its user but it is worth remembering that cartridges should not be stored in either a freezing cold garage during winter or left alongside the airing cupboard or radiators indoors. Nor should they be left to 'cook' for long periods inside a sun-heated car in summer.

Excessive heat can draw moisture out of the powder and cause it to burn more fiercely, thus raising pressures which, in very extreme cases, might affect pattern quality, while marrow-numbing cold will bring about an opposite reaction. It is for this reason that manufacturers who load for countries where extremes in temperature range are encountered will opt for more expensive double-based powders which can withstand wide fluctuations. It can be argued that in temperate climes there is little reason to spend a few extra pounds per thousand for cartridges loaded with such powder but the option is worth keeping if only for the confidence that comes through using a brand which you know to be absolutely consistent.

Whichever powder type is used by the loader the thing that is uppermost in his mind is how to match this to the other components and ensure that pattern quality remains high. By carefully balancing powder with the type of primer in use and the tightness of the crimp holding everything in place, the maker can control pressures generated inside the gun and also the velocity of the pellets emerging from the barrel. Too much powder can have a detrimental effect on the evenness of the pattern but when it comes to maintaining consistent spread at the ranges intended of the cartridge, the loader pays careful attention to the quality of pellets he uses.

If these are too soft a greater number will be distorted, first by the initial crush of ignition, followed by abrasion as they pass up the barrel and then by the 'squeezing' effect of any choke present in the gun. As misshapen pellets do not fly true and lose energy more quickly, the pattern will tend to spread too quickly, thinning in the process and making it an inconsistent performer at maximum ranges. Either the gaps in the pattern will allow the target to escape untouched or the few pellets which do cover it might be too weak actually to break it.

Such a cartridge might well be ideal for close-range work where maximum spread with sufficient pellet energy comes into its own but, if the intention is to produce one that remains consistently effective at maximum distances, our loader needs to look again at the problem. He does this by adding a hardening agent called antimony to the lead during the smelting process and in this way is able to reduce the incidence of damage when the powder goes to work. Loaders seeking optimum patterning quality not only add hardener but also carefully grade the shot they choose by ensuring that it is absolutely round before dropping it into the cartridge.

Also, just to make sure the shot does fly as true as possible after leaving the barrel, loaders might well spend time polishing it so that it cuts through the air with minimal air resistance. But even when all this has been done there is still something of a balancing act to be performed: choosing a shot size which is sufficiently large to retain plenty of 'killing' energy at outer ranges but which fills the pattern sufficiently well to ensure that the target will be struck.

The loader can increase this stopping power by choosing bigger and bigger shot but it should be noted that as the size goes up, fewer pellets can be loaded into the cartridge case with obvious consequences on the density – and hence strike rate – of the pattern. Nor is the answer to be found in filling the case with twice the number of tiny pellets. They might well fill the pattern satisfactorily but now the problem is one of energy: small pellets lose their striking power more quickly than large shot and will, in all probability, rattle off a target at maximum range without breaking it.

Shot Size

The rules of Sporting stipulate that shot larger than No. 6 and smaller than No. 9 cannot be used. This might sound as though it is far too narrow a band for manufacturers to work within but, in actual fact, the options available neatly cover clay shooting requirements. Shot sizes 7, 7½ and 8 are sufficient in energy and numbers to meet both energy and density demands. The smallest shot – No. 9 – fails as a long-distance load on energy grounds but when loaded with soft pellets for greater spread it represents an ideal proposition for targets at close to middle ranges.

The problem (if it can be called that) as far as the customer is concerned is in deciding which shot size to use against which target. Confidence, personal preference and, more important, past experience will largely dictate which to put into orbit. Unfortunately it is not possible to give a yardage equation where one shot starts to fail and another takes over because individual interpretation of range varies wildly; so much so that 35 yards to one might well appear as 25 yards or maybe even 45 yards to another – especially so when the target is thrown with nothing but the sky behind it to give any depth to distance.

Much too depends on the angle of the target and whether it is being presented edge-on or is showing some, or all, its thin, vulnerable centre. For my own part, I prefer to play safe and only use No. 9 shot (popularly called Skeet) on very close-range birds up to 20 yards. Beyond that – and certainly for clays that present nothing but their thick rim to the shooter – I plump for Trap 7½'s. It is tempting to think that the marginally wider spread of a skeet shell gives some leeway in aiming error, but for my money I would rather bank on energy to see the job done properly and not run the risk, however slight, of tickling the clay and not breaking it.

If there is a safe halfway house in this perplexing problem it comes in the shape of No. 8 shot which, in recent years, has grown enormously in popularity especially among people who favour open chokes. On the one hand, it has more than enough small pellets to fill the pattern and, on the other, it is big enough to carry breaking energy a long way. Anybody who doubts that it cannot shatter Sporting targets at exceptionally long distances would do well to look at some of the champions who use it to the exclusion of all others. Even at extreme range this pellet size has shown itself to have sufficient energy not only to break the target with seeming ease but also to crunch it up well and proper thanks to the density of pellets filling out the pattern.

So far we have touched briefly on the lateral spread of the pattern after it leaves the barrel and maybe it is as well to leave it at that. Anybody who wants to engross themselves in pellet counts, effective spreads, shot sizes, flyers and the rest will find plenty of literature in most libraries or book suppliers. Suffice it to say that as a rough guide the effective width of pattern can be said to widen at the rate of 1 inch per yard from the barrel. In other words, at 10 yards' distance the shot will span 10 inches, at 20 yards, 20 inches and so on up to 40 yards, a mark which is normally taken as being the outer effective distance for a shotgun to deliver optimum performance.

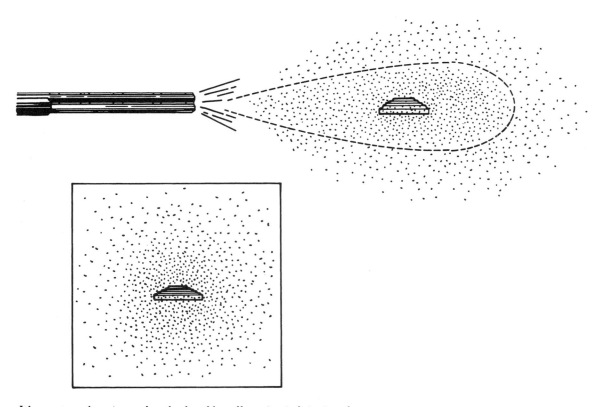

It's easy to underestimate the role played by pellet string in bringing about a successful shot. The way the target breaks often depends on where it passed through the shot cloud and this can give the observant shooter an idea of lead requirements for the next target. The pattern plate only tells half the story – but it can be useful in determining individual gun fit.

Shot Stringing

A 40-yard target, whether clay or the real thing, is a long shot by anybody's reckoning but No. 7, or 8, shot through a reasonable choke will break targets cleanly and consistently quite a way beyond this if the gun is held straight. In addition to lateral spread, the speeding pellets also demonstrate depth in the form of an elongated swarm which lengthens as the distance increases.

Tests show that even with good quality, round shot the length of this 'flying cylinder' can be as much as 12 to 15 feet at 40 yards; longer if the pellets are all different sizes or battered out of shape for the reasons given at the outset of the chapter. This is because misshapen shot not only flies on a path which takes it away from the aiming point but it also travels more slowly because of increased air resistance and loses speed much earlier than do the properly rounded pellets which are up front of the column. The cripples and walking wounded in the column lag ever farther behind.

Many great minds have pondered long and hard over this subject of shot stringing and each, in turn, has offered explanations about why some are longer than others, how the string can be shortened and what percentage likelihood there is of a target being dealt a telling blow by the weakened pellets bringing up the rear of the column. It is all very thought provoking. Yet one area where people love to disagree is whether stringing is a good, or bad, thing in terms of consistent strikes on a target.

There are two schools of thought on this. One argues that there is nothing to be gained in having a string which is over long because the rear two-thirds of the column are made up of underpowered pellets which behave inconsistently and so cannot be trusted. The short-string lobbyists maintain that good, clean and reliable breaks are the hallmark of a target being hit fair and square by the properly shaped pellets at the front of the column. The other school argues that long string is a highly desirable element, especially when it comes to shooting at targets which demand any amount of lead as, for example, in the case of long crossers. Even though it takes the entire retinue of pellets but a flickering second to pass the target there is a chance that, should the gun be slightly too far in front when the shot is fired, it will be broken by pellets bringing up the rear.

There is little doubt that well-shaped pellets delivering maximum energy and optimum pattern at the head of the string are responsible for the cleanest kills of all, but the tail-end Charlies should not be dismissed as wholly inconsistent strikers of the target. While excessively long stringing caused by poor quality pellets will leave the rear of a shot column so weakly populated that consistent hits will be unlikely in the event of a shooter over-leading a clay at long range, the stringing characteristics of a standard cartridge should be welcomed.

This is because no clay shooter can guarantee that he is so accurate as to be able to break the target every time with the first few pellets leading the 'charge' up range. If he were that good he should be able to hit them with cartridges loaded with solid ball! Of course, he would never thank you for coming out of the crowd and asking him to try a few. This is because targets are broken by a shooter placing the shot string in front of them and allowing the clay to run into the column of pellets. If we are skilful enough to catch the target in the densest part of the string a satisfying break caused by multiple hits will ensue, but the clay will be still marked down as 'killed' should it pass through the column's trailing edge and merely be hit in the chops and cracked in half by a couple of 'has beens'.

Such unspectacular breaks will never boost a shooter's confidence in the way that a pulverised clay can but at least he will gain some comfort from the probability that stringing was working for, not against, him on that occasion. String and the way it breaks the target, can also be a great ally in helping us determine how much – or little – lead the next clay tracking along the same path and at the same speed needs. The common sight of a target having its front or back edge shaved off tells us that the lead has been either overdone or undercooked and that a minor correction will put it in the densest part of the shot column next time for a more convincing kill.

Confidence in the notion that shot string works for, and not against, a shooter can be gained by anybody who bases his approach on Maintained Lead because he is using a style that benefits from the fact that clays are broken by flying into the shot cloud and not by being shot at. Keeping the gun ahead of the clay means that most of the string is working for him, especially in the event of fractionally too much forward allowance being imparted by the gun.

Choke

We have seen that the main cause of stringing is due to actual pellet quality but the degree of choke present in the barrel also has a marginal effect by elongating the shot charge as it squeezes past the constriction. Lateral spread might be reduced but the important element here is that the pellet cloud should be showing a greater degree of central concentration for most of its length and so deliver a slightly better strike rate wherever the target happens into the string. Few people would feel happy using a gun on Sporting clays with full choke in both barrels because the narrower spread of pellets places the onus on them to show greater accuracy on the target's line of flight, particularly on near-range birds. On far-away crossers, though, its centrally dense string is potent medicine indeed.

As ever, the choice of cartridge/choke combination is a matter of personal compromise, confidence and belief. You might dismiss the value of shot string in breaking the target as negligible. You might even feel that anything more than quarter and half choke is a confounded handicap. Everybody is entitled to

their own opinion and my own is that stringing is both an advantage and an ally well worth having. Furthermore, half choke in both barrels is a compromise which, I feel, gives adequate spread at all ranges and a workmanlike shot column at distances (and targets) where we need every bit of help we can get. How the string is presented to the target, of course, is a different matter, one which relies on nothing more, nor less, than our own shooting technique.

Apart from taking note of the stated hardness of the pellets loaded into cartridges, it is not possible to measure the actual length of the shot string unless you want to go to the time, trouble and expense of setting up a big pattern plate on the side of a lorry and shooting at it as the vehicle trundles past. If cartridge performance interests you that much then by all means go ahead and engross yourself in the subject. The results will keep you busy for hours! But, returning to our earlier observations about cartridge consistency, it really is enough to know that modern shells will break the target as long as our technique has done its bit. The way it breaks when covered by the string is the real acid test. Try several different brands to see if any one – or more – appears to do the job better. If they do, it is reasonably safe to assume that out of your gun and choke their string and patterning characteristics are as good as you could hope for.

One visual test that can be done to assure yourself that any given cartridge in a particular gun is working to full potential is to 'pattern' it against a flat metal sheet carrying an aiming mark. This can be either whitewashed or covered in paper to record the pellet hits. Occasionally, some guns will throw patterns which do not match up to their nominal borings but, in the main, modern cartridges will turn in pellet counts pretty close to the percentages expected of them. If the patterns do not appear to match up by all means note how one cartridge differs from another, but the intention of this test is to check that the choke is not throwing a 'lop-

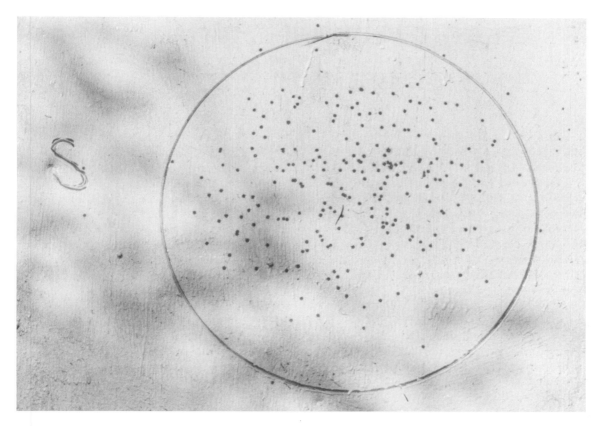

There is little point patterning your gun and cartridge unless you are unhappy about the way it breaks the target. The pattern plate is better used as a means of checking gun fit and that the shotgun shoots where you look.

'sided' pattern or one that does not align with the aiming point.

If you find that the centre of the spread appears to be going consistently right, left, high or low of the mark, get a couple of friends to fire the gun and see if they get the same results. If they do not, it might probably indicate that you are not mounting the gun properly or that it is not a correct fit. Let us assume that it is. You are covering the aiming mark but most of the pellets are showing a regular tendency to 'crowd' away from this in a particular corner of the plate. And it does not change, regardless of cartridge being fired. If such unevenness does manifest itself, the gun should be checked by a practical gunsmith who will, by polishing out part of the choke, be able to correct the imbalance and bring the pellets back to where they belong.

Such imbalances do not crop up too often but even so it is worth satisfying yourself that your gun is not one of the few. Once you have cleared away all doubts about the physical performance of your choke you can rest assured that the cartridge is capable of looking after itself. All you need concern yourself with is sorting out your technique!

5 Driven Clays – High, Low, Fast and Slow

There is no such thing as an easy clay pigeon. Shooting grounds are awash with people (me included!) who could have done better if only they had not missed so many stupidly simple targets during their practice or competition round. The language used to describe such frustration is normally a little sharper and more direct, of course, but the sentiment is one everybody will be able to identify with. After all, how many times have you smashed all the difficult birds only to walk away from a stand of sitters shaking your head and wondering how you could possibly have missed such heaven-sent opportunities?

Straightforward driven targets are a classic example. If the shooting course is a particularly difficult one you can almost see the relief in shooters' faces when they arrive at a gentle driven stand. They have been made to work really hard on the previous five or six stations but now they can relax a little bit, the next five pairs are as good as 'in the bag'. Nobody can possibly miss them . . .

Yet driven birds do not have to be very high or very fast to turn the shooter inside out. Indeed, the easier they look, the greater is the danger of the shooter coming unstuck.

This will no doubt strike people as something of an oddity. After all, don't shooting instructors invariably start novices off on driven birds just because they are the easiest of all targets to hit? They most certainly do. But what people tend to forget is that while driven birds are easy things to break and so confidence building in those days, they also underline for the novice the need to recognise target speed and flight characteristics from the very outset and encourage him to mount and move the gun smoothly.

We will stay with the novice for the time being because the errors he will doubtless commit are the very same as those that an experienced performer will make if he allows himself to take the target for granted.

It can be seen that for any target except one thrown directly at the shooter's head some degree of forward allowance is going to be needed to put the shot and clay on a collision course. With Follow-Through this is achieved by bringing a mounted gun from behind the oncoming target and squeezing the trigger as the muzzles sweep passed the clay's leading edge. Needless to say, a clay passing 40 yards overhead is going to need twice as much forward allowance as one travelling the same speed 20 yards lower so the Follow-Through shooter has either to increase his lead on the higher bird by swinging through it faster and firing as he passes the clay or else he has to delay pulling the trigger until the gun has moved well in front.

With a little experience, a competent shooter gets to know fairly instinctively how quickly he needs to swing the gun and when he should squeeze the trigger, but if his timing should be slightly out or he misreads the target's speed, then a miss is not only possible, it is a near certainty.

Experience helps no matter what shooting style is followed but at least with Maintained Lead the shooter avoids the numerous pitfalls that revolve round the changing fortunes of barrel speed in relation to the height and rate of travel of a target like this.

Eye-to-hand co-ordination helps to ensure that the gun matches its speed to that of the target so a shooter does not have to worry about 'hanging fire' until the relationship of

A trick shooter shows how simple eye-to-hand co-ordination will bring the gun muzzles to the right position ahead of a target every time.

barrel to target matches up to any mental pictures he might have formed through previous experience, nor will he have to make conscious changes to the speed of the gun to impart the right forward allowance. By allowing his eyes to direct the gun, a Maintained Lead shooter will automatically bring the muzzles to the right position ahead of the clay.

The golden rule with any target that you choose to shoot by maintaining the lead is to ensure that the gun muzzles are never held too far back on its line of flight so that the clay catches, or overtakes, the gun during the Move, Mount, Shoot sequence. To prevent this from happening the shooter must be clear on two points: where he plans to break the clay and where he will get his first, clear view of it after it has left the trap. Once this has been determined, the muzzles of the unmounted gun should be addressed to the mid-point.

A common mistake among people trying Maintained Lead for the first time is to rush the gun to the shoulder as soon as they see the clay and then try to maintain a constant lead before firing. This is both unnecessary and undesirable. For a start, the eye uses the gap between the target's 'entry' point and the unmounted gun muzzles to register its line of flight and speed automatically. By mounting too soon, the shooter not only interferes with this process but also allows the clay to close the gap, forcing him to jerk the gun in an attempt to stay ahead of it. All too often the target gets past anyway, thus leaving the shooter no option but to chase, overtake and shoot it in much the same way as a Follow-Through shooter would.

Reacting too quickly to the driven target can be a hard habit to break but unless the sportsman slows down and gives his reflex actions a chance to work properly he will never reap the full rewards that await him.

In this respect, the three instructions – Move, Mount, Shoot – would do better to read Mmmmove, Mmmount, Ssshoot: in other words, the gun starts to Mmmmove

when the target is seen properly and is Mmmounted securely just before the shot is fired. The three instructions should be blended into one smooth package and never split. The whole operation is silky smooth.

It cannot be repeated often enough that the speed of the gun barrel will take its cue directly from the speed of the bird so please do not worry about mounting the gun only to find that the target has outfoxed you and gone past the muzzle. The only way it will have done this is if you have looked in the wrong place for the bird, taken your barrels too far back to the trap or checked your swing. Provided you Mmmmove when you see the target, there should be little danger of the gun slowing or stopping in this fashion.

If the gun was mounted without interruption and you do miss, chances are the target will have been missed in front. It is rare indeed to miss behind unless you actually stop the gun, so if you do not connect adjust your barrel-hold position by moving a little nearer to the target's entry point.

POSTURE AND WEIGHT DISTRIBUTION

One thing which you must bear in mind with any driven bird (and this applies regardless of the shooting style you use) is whether it needs to be shot off the front or back foot. The determining factor here is the speed of the clay and the amount of time you have to mount the gun and fire the shot.

If, for argument's sake, the clay appears over a belt of trees and very quickly disappears overhead, it will probably have to be shot with the gun in a near-perpendicular position. If this is the case, the shooter will make things harder for himself by trying to shoot such a bird with his weight on the front foot. Such a stance makes it difficult to keep the gun moving when it reaches the vertical position because our physical limitations mean that our arms and back reach a point where they cannot move any further. When

Place your gun muzzles between where you will see the target clearly and where you want to break it. Fight the urge to mount as soon as the clay appears.

John demonstrates the correct way to shoot a driven bird off the leading foot out in front. His gun addresses the mid-point and he looks back for the clay.

His eyes are still on the clay and he has started to Move and Mount the gun.

The gun is now shouldered and the shot taken without undue delay.
Note that the weight is still over the front foot, cancelling out any
tendency to lift the head off the stock.

56

By raising his left heel and transferring his weight smoothly to the back leg, John is able to move the gun through the perpendicular and maintain his lead on the second bird of a simultaneous pair.

57

this point is reached the gun will come to a quite definite stop, causing the shot to miss behind.

Valuable extra swing can be achieved by placing the weight on the back foot and allowing the spine to bend and take the arms beyond the perpendicular. In terms of muzzle movement such a transfer of weight might only achieve a couple of feet of extra travel at ground level but in terms of up-range lead it corresponds to a vast amount of sky in which the target can be broken.

Raising the heel of the front foot while the weight is shifted to the rear helps to improve upper-body mobility and this is one habit worth cultivating in the quiet of your own home whenever you indulge in a spot of dry mounting. Time spent this way is never wasted, especially if you teach yourself to shift the distribution of weight from the front to back foot in one movement. At some shooting ground or other you will eventually come up against a pair of driven targets that encourage you to take the first shot out in front but then leave you struggling to maintain gun movement directly overhead for the second target. In this situation, you need to be able to move easily on to the back leg to get off a second, controlled, shot and so break the pair comfortably.

With a little bit of practice most shooters will become quite proficient at doing this but be on your guard against developing the horrible habit of drooping the right shoulder and rolling your head to the right once the gun is reaching the vertical position. A trait like this is normally born of a lazy gun mount and is symptomatic of a shooter 'sitting' on his rear hip. The stock will rarely come to rest in the shoulder pocket but instead will probably take up position on the arm socket, causing the shot to miss to the left of the target while the head will end up anywhere but in the right position on the comb and the master eye will pull the gun muzzles with it.

It is important that a Sporting clays shooter gets used to transferring his weight from one leg to the other on tower birds because when it comes to shooting targets thrown from behind it is weight transfer that helps break them more than anything else.

I have satisfied myself that with Maintained Lead most misses are normally in front of the target but this going-away overhead bird is one which can all too easily reverse the trend. The problem is caused by the fact that the target is now going in the opposite direction to that of our natural gun mount which is upward.

It is a tricky target which, if care is not taken, will encourage the shooter to lift the gun to his face and shoulder in the normal way and then force him to change the gun's direction of momentum and chase after it. More complications set in because 'forward allowance' as we like to picture it ceases to exist if the target is allowed to get too far away before the trigger is squeezed. To the shooter an overhead clay like this appears to be travelling downward and, as the distance increases, it goes from being a full-view target overhead to one that is edge-on well away from the shooting station.

The longer we leave this clay the more we are likely to put ourselves on the slippery slope of inconsistency; we now hope that by shooting somewhere underneath the target we will manage to clip it with the shot string.

Low, going-away birds, often have to be killed edge on but, in the case of targets being thrown from a higher tower, we usually have sufficient time to see the belly of the clay and get our barrels in front to break it. To do this we must adopt a technique which moves the gun with the target's line of flight, not against it.

This is achieved by paying very close attention to weight distribution and how it is transferred from one foot to the other. For a start, the weight should be placed on the back foot and the body arched to allow us to pick up the target as soon as possible overhead. Remember as well the need to decide where the target should be broken and make sure you hold the unmounted gun muzzles on a mid-point along its flight path. Do not be

Smooth transfer of weight from back to front leg is the only sure way of maintaining lead in front of a target driven from behind. Note the arched body, gun tucked against the rib-cage and raised left heel.

As soon as the bird appears, the shooter starts transferring the weight from one leg to the other. This ensures that the gun muzzles travel with the line of the target, not against it.

60

The shooter's weight is now going on to the left leg and the right heel is being raised. The muzzles are still moving ahead of the target as the stock comes into the shoulder.

Weight transfer is completed just as the gun is firmly bedded into the face and shoulder. The gun is fired without delay.

Top Belgian shooter Marc Polet decides he wants to pick up the clay off this high tower as soon as possible. He obviously does not suffer from a bad back!

tempted to hold the gun at too steep an angle because to do so will allow the target time to pass the line of the barrels and so force you to start chasing down from behind.

The aim of this particular exercise is to make sure the gun starts in front and stays there. This is done quite neatly by gradually shifting the weight from the back foot to the front as the gun is being mounted. In essence, this is a gentle rocking motion which starts as soon as the target comes into view from behind and is not completed until the gun has been securely mounted into the cheek and shoulder. Do not fall into the trap of trying to shoot too quickly because to do so will encourage a jerky gun mount and lead to the gun being 'poked' at the target and missing it behind.

Overhead tower birds like this are not too difficult to hit but it does pay to spend time getting the basics right by dry mounting at home and putting theory into practice down on the shooting range whenever you can. I suppose the secret of hitting these targets consistently is one of timing but this is something which will come with practice and experience.

Once you can master this 'back to front' shooting technique by polishing the subtle rhythm of weight transfer then this target can be tackled with great confidence. But, as with tower birds driven towards the shooter, care needs to be taken that by placing weight over the back foot the shoulder and head do not roll. If they do, the gun will come off the clay's line of flight every time no matter how hard you try to mount the gun properly.

So far we have only looked at tower targets thrown straight over the shooter's head, yet more often than not the man who lays out the course will try to present them so they pass to one side or other of the shooting station; some might pass just over the shoulder while others could be thrown as wide crossing birds; they might even be thrown at an angle whereby they quarter into, or away from, the shooter. The permutations are many and varied – more so if they also come as pairs travelling in different directions from two, separate, traps!

Regardless of height, speed and direction the techniques already described can be brought into play with every chance of success. However, great care needs to be exercised in adjusting your stance to take account of the different angles.

There is little point, after all, setting yourself up as if to shoot a target coming directly overhead when, instead, it is going to pass several yards to one side. All you will manage to achieve is an ever-restricted gun movement to the point where you can no longer maintain lead in any shape or form. The golden rule then is always to adopt a stance which allows the barrels to be brought into the bird's line of flight and stay on it after the shot has been taken.

This is particularly important in the case of doubles from separate traps because to stand a fair chance of breaking both birds the shooter will have to adjust his foot position in a way that brings him into the second target easily. This might also mean taking one bird off the front foot, turning slightly for the other and having to drop on to the back foot to shoot it directly overhead. As such, it is important that the shooter not only recognises the challenge presented by the birds on offer before stepping on to the shooting station, but that he has also practised his footwork to the point where the adjustments become second nature.

Anybody who already has a reasonable amount of experience of the driven target in its various guises will need to make only minor improvements to his technique to overcome problematic angles. However, beginners would be better advised to map out their progress by mastering low, slow incomers first before eventually moving on to high, fast and angled targets. Progress will be made quickly by anybody who sets about the task methodically; the aim is to build confidence to a level where the sportsman can enter an open competition and not feel overawed by the targets that will come his way.

This high tower at Roundwood in Hampshire is regarded as being one of the highest, and hardest, in the land. On the day this photograph was taken the traps had been set to throw a fast, 50-yard crossing bird – a severe test for any shooting technique and shooter.

Beware slow targets which come to a virtual standstill overhead. They encourage the shooter to shift his weight to the back leg and lift his head from the stock in the process.

Now is probably an opportune time to return to our experienced group of shooters thanking the Lord for what they are about to receive after struggling round much of the earlier course. They could well be in for a nasty shock.

Clay shooting punishes anybody who takes a target for granted and this is especially so of driven targets ambling along in seductive fashion. The worst ones are those which can be seen in plenty of time and even hang in the air after losing most of their forward momentum. In such cases it is easy to allow yourself to stop the swing of the gun as you make sure of the sacrificial offering and also lift your head from the stock to get a better look at it as it floats toward you. Never underestimate the ability of such a bird to force a shooter into all sorts of errors – the worst being head lifting and drifting on to the back foot when it should, instead, be attacked off the left leg out in front.

6 Coping with Crossers

Consistency in clay pigeon shooting means many things to many men but in the end it boils down to little more than an ability on the part of the shooter to remember a drill and, bit by bit, build up his confidence by breaking targets he knows he can hit before moving on to even more testing birds.

Confidence is the key to the whole learning process: confidence in the gun and equipment, in the way you stand and mount the gun and in the drill you follow.

Some people, of course, learn faster than others and it is not unusual to find that of two friends who started together, one will be much farther advanced than the other in the types of target he will happily tackle. One will be eager to find grounds that throw targets his usual clubs cannot provide while his companion might well be still struggling on some that the other no longer finds a challenge.

In the early days it is part of the fun and learning process to shoot as many different targets as possible without worrying too much about whether they are hit or missed. However, often it is what happens after the initial introduction has been made that dictates how quickly – or slowly – each individual shooter develops.

Total novices realise that a course of shooting lessons at the very outset is a desirable introduction to the sport and will soak up as much information as possible during each session and try to reproduce some, if not all, of those new-found skills at a convenient shooting ground between visits. This is as it should be. Yet from the instructor's point of view it is interesting to note which of his pupils return to the 'classroom' having had time to do some shooting and identify problem targets. Such people show an obvious desire

to do well and they set about their difficulties in a structured and thoughtful manner.

As for the others, a small number may have mastered the subject in double-quick time and will be next seen at the shooting school doing quite well in open competition. But by far the biggest number will have taken themselves off to all four corners of the county to struggle along under their own steam enjoying some success on the way but not really getting on top of the targets that cause them the greatest problems. No doubt limited budgets rule out additional lessons for many but more often than not it is the 'I have been shown how it should be done and now it's down to me' attitude that stops people coming back.

Whatever the reason, if a novice does decide to 'go it alone' it must be borne in mind that the best way to improve proficiency is to set about problematic targets in a methodical manner. Progress will be slowed if the shooter fails to isolate his weaknesses and show a willingness to tackle them one at a time.

In this respect, I recall meeting trap and skeet shooters who had singled out specific angles and stations where they habitually came unstuck and diligently practised on one particular target until they were satisfied they had got the measure of it. Often it was solved by shifting their stance slightly or adopting a different hold position in relation to the trap house or line of flight. How they overcame their difficulties is not really the issue here; rather the fact that they were not only prepared to recognise their shortcomings but were keenly determined to find a solution that could be accommodated within their basic technique. Very many more Sporting shooters could benefit by showing similar devotion to detail.

*Novices and inexperienced shooters can learn a great deal simply by
watching how a proficient performer tackles crossing birds, in this case
shooting instructor Terry King from Leicester.*

RECOGNISING PROBLEMS

Little progress will be made by anybody who
bangs away with mixed success at whatever
targets are on offer at his club's Sunday
morning get-together and then puts away his
gun – and thoughts – until the following
fortnight when he will go through the same
old routine again. Self-improvement will follow only if he would admit to himself that he
has difficulties with certain targets or angles
and then sets about tackling the problem.

If you feel as though you are in the 'going
nowhere fast' category it will help to make a
list of the birds that cause the most problems.
List too the ones that you can hit consistently.
Go back to your club during practice hours

and concentrate on working through the list
one problem at a time and move on to the
next only when you feel that you have solved
the first one.

There is no shame in tackling a problem in
this fashion. Even the best shots in the country take themselves off to a quiet corner of a
shooting ground or farmer's field to sharpen
up on those targets that they do not always
break as confidently as they would like. This
is especially so after a set-back at a big shoot
where, had they only broken one or two more
specific targets, they would have probably
won a prize. It has happened to everyone.

My most painful 'if only' memory centred
on a World Sporting Championship in Switzerland during the 1970s. I finished up being

beaten in seventh place, and, of the targets I missed during the four-day shoot, thirteen were rabbits! As soon as I got back home, I went straight to my local club and shot rabbit targets from every conceivable angle, distance and speed until I felt happy that I had solved the problem: in this instance, shooting with a stance that was too upright caused me to miss over the top.

Different targets, though, perplex different shooters so it is not always possible to list the angles most likely to cause problems in a descending scale of difficulty. However, if we look at it from a beginner's point of view it is probably that at the top of most lists would be the crossing bird. This is not very surprising because it is the one that, with a high driven target, demands the greatest amount of forward allowance of any bird encountered on a shooting range. Close-range skeet-type targets are bad enough for a great number of people, but add extra distance and height and the problems for anybody who dreads a crosser can multiply alarmingly.

Hopefully, crossers do not fill you with the same fear and trembling that some poor souls suffer when confronted with this type of target, yet please spare a thought for them. It is no exaggeration to say that some of the people that have booked lessons with me have been frozen rigid by the mere sight of them. And these include some very accomplished shooters who, quite simply, have hit a bad patch by allowing themselves to take on board a number of bad habits in their ever more frantic attempts to solve their problems.

These problems, though, can usually be traced back to a simple fault in basic style – incorrect stance and gun hold head the list. These are so easy to put right that some people actually feel embarrassed at having travelled maybe 100 miles or more only to have the fault corrected within the space of a 25 carton of cartridges. Some, of course, are not so easily cured. The fault will be spotted almost immediately but trying to get the customer to shed a habit that, with time, has

become deeply ingrained can prove decidedly awkward. However, provided the pupil is willing to learn, progress will, eventually, be made.

It is clear from this that what is needed above all else is a system that a shooter can rely on to deliver the goods; one he can go straight back to if things start to go wrong and on which he can reassure himself that most faults are minor and able to be cured by him alone.

We talked earlier about positioning ourselves properly for the shot and how the gun barrels assumed the mid-position between where we first see the target clearly and where it will be broken. Let us then, for ease of practice, take Station Four high-house skeet as a training aid and use what we learn there as a basis for every other crossing target – high, low, near and far – to be found around the Sporting range.

Forget all about Helpful Harry standing right behind telling you that this bird needs killing over the centre peg with two feet of lead. You are going to break it with eye-to-hand co-ordination so tell him, politely, to clear off and do not make a start until he is safely back in the clubhouse. Take up the ready stance by pointing the front foot to where you plan to break the target (if that is over the centre peg, so be it) and transfer some of your weight over the front leg to help ensure that when the stock is mounted your head stays comfortably on the comb of the gun.

Now pivot from your hips back along the target's line of flight to the gun hold point and then look even further back to where you will get your first clear view of the clay after it has left the trap. Do not be tempted to take the gun barrels this far back because if you do the target will pass the muzzles, forcing you to chase it up from behind. The actual gun hold position in relation to the target's actual line of flight is not exactly crucial at this stage but it is preferable to hold the muzzles just underneath it so that the clay can be kept in view all the time and the gun

John has placed his feet and pivoted back to the gun hold position. He is now looking further back to where the clay will come clearly into view.

The target has reached the point of no return. The gun barrels respond by moving along in front. John's eyes remain fixed to the clay.

By the time the gun starts to come up to the shoulder, the eyes and hands have directed the muzzles into position and the pivoting body ensures that the lead is maintained.

The gun is now fully mounted and all that remains is for the trigger to be squeezed. Note the position of John's leading leg – there is still plenty of swing in there if it is needed.

brought up and into its path. You might feel happier matching the muzzles more closely to the line but, whatever you do, avoid holding too high because this will obscure your view of the clay and encourage you to chop down on the bird at the last moment. This is a bad habit and should be nipped in the bud from the outset.

Providing you have taken up the right position with your feet and barrel hold, the actual shot will be something of a formality. This is not to say that you should take it for granted. By forcing yourself to concentrate on the target you will ensure that eye-to-hand co-ordination will bring the gun easily into position ahead of it. All that now remains is to squeeze the trigger and keep the gun moving until the clay has broken.

TIMING

Do not be in too much of a hurry to get the gun stock to the shoulder. This is easier said than done if you have been used to shooting all your targets up until now with a Follow-Through style because, as we have seen, part of the technique is to close the gap between where you hold the gun and where you pick up the target. In the case of this skeet bird, a Follow-Through shooter would probably recommend holding the gun a foot or two out from the trap house, looking back to the chute of the trap itself and mounting as soon as the target appears, the mounted gun then being swept quickly along its path and fired as the muzzles pass its leading edge.

One very worthwhile advantage of Maintained Lead is that with a little practice most shooters get to know where they miss targets as well as knowing how they missed. This concept is particularly hard to grasp for somebody raised on a diet of Follow-Through because too much rests on the speed of swing. Too fast and the shot can miss in front, too slow and it will miss behind.

The only people I have met who use Follow-Through and are able to say with a degree of

accuracy where they missed are those with a lot of shooting experience. The rest always seem to exhibit a degree of uncertainty which is not shown by a Maintained Lead shooter of more limited experience. This is quite easy to understand as this method puts the gun ahead of the target and so most misses will naturally be in front. Other benefits also accrue under this system. With experience, the Maintained Lead shooter also learns to develop an instinctive ability to know when he has shot over, and under, the bird and can so form a mental yardstick of sorts on which to work for the next shot.

This does not mean, of course, that there will not be times when the target is missed behind. And, strange as it may seem, a Maintained Lead shooter who does miss in this fashion will likely as not be unable to say where he placed the shot. At least such confusion does provide its own answer and so steps can be taken to remedy the mistake.

The most common cause for a miss behind is an incorrect hold position before the target is called. Either the gun has been taken too far back along the line of flight and the target has managed to get too close to the muzzles before the shooter started to Move, or, he held too far out, started to Move and then slowed (or stopped) the Mount momentarily when he realised his mistake. Another cause is turning the body too far into the target and thus running out of swing when the gun starts to come into the face and shoulder. This, as we have already seen, causes the muzzles to slow involuntarily.

The consequences of an incorrect stance will be felt by the shooter because the gun mount will feel restricted in its final stages, causing him to hang on the trigger longer than he would like as he tries to correct by flicking the gun ahead. In really bad cases the gun will stop altogether, in which case the reason will be all too apparent.

With a little experience, a shooter will find himself adopting the correct foot position almost automatically, but do please note the use of the word almost – even the most clay-

The same technique used on a head-height crossing bird at 20 yards works just as well on 40-yard crossers from a tower. Work out where you are going to break the clay, get into position and then look back for the target.

The gun is now starting to move . . .

74

. . . and takes it cue from the speed of the bird. The amount of lead has been established . . .

. . . and all that remains is for the gun to be fired as soon as the stock has been securely mounted.

hardened campaigners benefit by briefly double-checking their stance in relation to the line of flight before committing themselves and calling for the target. It is a routine which the less experienced would do well to copy.

If you have not yet reached that happy stage where stance and gun mount are virtually second nature, or you have slight doubts about the speed of the target, then it always pays to play safe and shift the toes of that front foot an inch or two further round from where you hope to break the clay. In this way you can guarantee valuable extra swing on a target that demands its full complement of gun movement and forward allowance.

The need for more and yet more forward allowance increases, of course, as the distance between shooter and target opens out. Yet anybody who can confidently break mid-range crossers will have few problems when he comes to tackle birds at greater range. The real difficulty is in convincing him that they are no harder than the others. In fact, some long targets are actually easier because they take longer to cross the shooter's front and, as such, give him valuable extra time to deal with them effectively.

The most common mistake when it comes to long crossers is one of trying to maintain the lead with a gun that has been mounted too quickly. This is doomed to cause inconsistency because it encourages the shooter to take his eyes away from the target while he picks a spot out in front to shoot at. At best, this encourages the shooter to pull away from such targets with an accelerating gun; at worst, it fosters the awful habit of poking the barrels at the clay because he is not completely sure how far in front he needs to be.

What our shooter has conveniently forgotten from his practice sessions on 20-yard birds is that the simple eye-to-hand co-ordination which brought the barrels into position ahead of this target will do the same

on one 30 or 40 yards away as well. In other words, as long as he positions himself properly and addresses the gun to the mid-point, he can let the apparent speed of the clay dictate the speed at which he moves the muzzles, mounts the gun and shoots. By controlling the urge to mount too quickly he is better able to turn his full attention to the target, allowing the eyes more time to absorb the information about its flight and pass this to the hands that point and control the gun.

When clubhouse talk comes down to crossers it is not uncommon to hear right-handed shooters say that they are sometimes aware of having to give left to right targets more lead than they do to ones travelling the other way at the same speed. Similarly, left-handed shooters say the same about right to left targets. On the face of it, this notion will surely strike any mathematicians among us as being decidedly odd: pure logic dictates that targets travelling at the same speed and distance as one another but in opposite directions require exactly the same lead – and so they do.

Yet, strange as it may seem, the lead picture on crossing targets can appear different to somebody who is in the habit of bringing his gun from behind the target, much more so than somebody who habitually uses Maintained Lead.

There is nothing at all sinister about this. It amounts to little more than an optical illusion created by the shooter's stance and the ease (in the case of the right-hander) with which he can move the gun from left to right rather than right to left. With a left to right target his mounted gun is moving quite easily and in a direction which takes the gun away from the body and face whereas with the other bird the gun has to be mounted 'against the grain', so to speak. To counteract this problem, the tendency is to swing the gun a little bit faster as the trigger is squeezed. In the process the lead appears to have been reduced. It has not been reduced, of course. It is just the same.

7 Beating the Incomer

Clay shooters can be a disbelieving group at times. This is especially so when it comes to persuading them that long overdue improvements to their standard of marksmanship can be gained if only they would take on board small modifications to the technique they have nurtured and protected for such a very long time. It goes without saying that the longer somebody has been shooting and doing his own thing the harder it is to convince him that there might be better, and more efficient, ways of getting results.

It is hard enough trying to convince a sportsman raised on a diet of Follow-Through that, just maybe, Maintained Lead holds an answer or two to targets he normally struggles to hit consistently. The last thing any coach would want to do is change a shooter's technique if it already produces results. What he will try to do (if his pupil has an open mind) is to add to his understanding if problems are encountered and guide him through the difficulties that bar the path to better all-round performances. If this means shooting Maintained Lead in preference to Follow-Through on problematic angles (or vice versa) then so be it. It is all part of the learning curve.

Watch a group of very good shots in action and the chances are you will notice that on any given stand each will tackle it differently. You might have to look closely to spot the differences. Nevertheless, they will be there: one might hold his gun muzzles a little bit farther back than somebody else, another could be standing slightly squarer to the target while others might favour to hold over, under (or on) the target's line of flight. One might prefer to shoot Maintained Lead on crossing birds yet prefer to bring the gun from behind on any that have a tendency to quarter away from him. Another might maintain lead on the quarterers and follow through with the crossers, and so on.

The lesson to be drawn from this is that these successful practitioners have developed their styles, likes and dislikes by trial and error. They have been prepared to adopt different ideas when the need has arisen, tried them out, rejected those that do not work for them and held on to those that do.

The purpose of this book is to explain how Sporting targets can be broken in a consistent manner with Maintained Lead but this does not mean that each shooter should not make up his own mind and adapt points of technique to his own style if, perchance, he finds that the unexpurgated version does not work as well for him as he had hoped. A point in case is the incoming dropper.

A common name for this on the shooting course is the 'Duck' or 'Settling Crow' stand, a clay that is thrown toward the shooter but, as it loses forward momentum starts to drop and floats down to earth. In its simplest form it can come within a few yards of the shooting position, either directly in front of the shooter or, more usually, to one side as a left or right quartering bird. But it can be thrown so that it drops to ground a lot farther out. Even long-range droppers of this sort can appear to be reasonably easy propositions, but it is the fact that they do look so easy that makes them so potentially difficult. The moment somebody starts to say to themselves 'Now here's a real dolly to have a go at' is the time to be on guard because a number of bad habits will come bubbling to the surface. And the faults that crop up really are stunningly basic – stopping the gun movement, head lifting and measuring the lead to make sure of the bird. And 'easy' birds like this can force even the most experienced Sporting

Right: the gun stock is firmly bedded into the face and shoulder and will result in the shot going where the shooter is looking.

Wrong: the face is brushing the comb of the gun and the head has been lifted to watch the incoming target. The shot will go high and left.

shot into the most amazing lapses of concentration.

A fine example of this peculiar trait came at a World Championship shoot in Portugal back in the mid-1980s. The course organisers decided to site a couple of automatic traps way out in the middle of a field and throw targets toward the waiting competitor. Each shooter had plenty of time to see the bird – it was visible from the moment it left the trap 70 yards away and seemed to take ages to fight its way against a stiff breeze. Most of the time it was held back on the wind and would drop a long, long way out from the shooter's position. This made things decidedly tricky, but those which did carry as intended came almost up to the firing point. This made life a little easier, but not much judging by the number that were missed . . . with both barrels!

It was interesting (and not a little amusing) to hear some spectators behind the shooting line quietly laying friendly wagers on whether the shooter in action would hit or miss the next lumbering clay floating in towards him. Yet the outcome was not hard to predict, especially when the competitor mounted his gun long before the clay came into range and started to ride it out in readiness. A miss invariably followed. Yet those who waited patiently until the clay made up its mind and then mounted and fired in one easy movement killed it more often than not, even when it was still 45 yards away and dropping like a stone.

It is because the sportsman can normally see this bird coming from a long way off that problems arise. The temptation to mount the gun too early, track the bird in and try to measure out how much downward lead it needs at the same time is overpoweringly strong. But it must be resisted. Steel yourself by deciding where you want to break the clay and put your feet into a position which will allow you to do so without checking the swing. By all means watch the target come all the way but do make a conscious decision to build an imaginary 'fence post' at a point

in its flight before which you steadfastly refuse to move the gun. Once this point has been established, hold the gun midway between the 'barrier' and the point at which the clay will break. Ensure too that the muzzles are well under its line. As soon as the target passes that imaginary line move the gun, mount and shoot. Do not delay and do not worry about the clay's rate of descent. Do not worry either about its lack of forward speed if it is quartering in to you. Put your trust in eye-to-hand co-ordination to match the speed of the gun to that of the clay and also to work out the correct forward allowance. All a shooter needs to do is make sure that he mounts the gun properly and fires as soon as everything is firmly bedded in.

So far so good. But how, we hear you ask, can the eye direct the moving gun into position under the target as well? We will come to this in just a moment but for now just trust in your eye's ability to calculate correctly and simply ensure that the muzzles are held below the target's line of flight when it crosses the 'barrier'. We are striving to bring the gun up – and into – the target rather than down on it. Bringing a gun up to a dropping bird might sound like a half-baked idea but it is not as strange as it appears: it is certainly nowhere near as difficult as bringing the muzzles down to it before trying to get underneath and then squeezing the trigger. You can prove it to your own satisfaction by trying the following simple test.

Pick an aiming mark a few yards in front and point your right index finger at it by quickly raising and extending your arm in one upward and outward movement. Where is it pointing? Assuming that you are a right-handed shooter with a right master eye, the tip of the aiming finger will come to rest in line with, and fractionally under, the chosen bull's-eye. (If it does not and comes to rest to the left of the mark you have stumbled on why you are missing much more than you hit – the left eye is taking over from the right and pulling the gun muzzles with it. To correct the fault you will either have to learn to shoot

The target is coming from a trap out of picture and will go to the shooter's right. He will not start moving the gun until the clay has passed his imaginary fence post. The gun muzzles are under the line of flight.

The clay has cleared the boundary 'post' and has reached the summit of its travel. The gun is being mounted. The muzzles are still under the bird.

The target is now dropping rapidly but note the position of the barrels under – and in front – of the clay.

The shot has been taken and the clay breaks into a cloud of dust. Note how the muzzles have 'flipped' up under recoil.

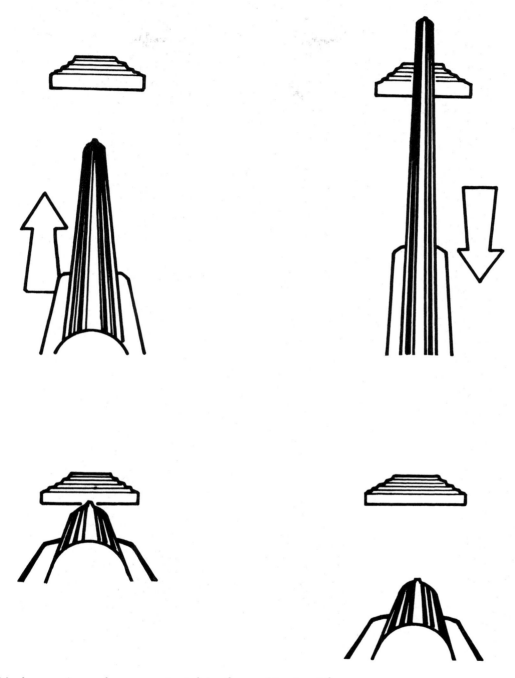

It's always easier – and more accurate – to bring the gun up to a target than it is to let the clay drift under the barrels and then try to get down and through it.

from the left shoulder, have a stock built to accommodate the sighting characteristic or, quite simply, learn to dim, or shut, the left eye just as the stock is being mounted to cancel out its domineering influence.

Now hold your extended arm above head height, look hard at the target and drop your arm and extended finger equally quickly to the chosen mark. Try as you might you will not be able to stop your finger on the mark. Instead it will finish up well under the mark rather than on it, as happened when the arm was brought up to the target. You can, if you like, substitute the extended finger for your usual gun. Mount the gun by bringing it up to the mark which now will sit comfortably on the rib and then hold the muzzles a few feet above it and try dropping, and mounting, the gun to the target. Try as you might, you will not be able to stop the barrels coming to rest well underneath the aiming point.

Don't fool yourself that because the target is dropping such a downward movement should be cultivated – it should not. The test you have just undertaken resulted in the imaginary shot missing the mark underneath – and the target was not even moving! It might seem the most natural thing to shoot a dropping target with a dropping gun but to do so in practice multiplies the chances of the target being missed underneath.

The fact that incoming droppers like this are losing height means, of course, that they are also losing speed. Some will be at a virtual standstill by the time the shooter has got the gun to his shoulder and is good and ready to squeeze the trigger. It is very noticeable that when a target like this hoves into range there is a tendency to stop the gun on it. It is almost as if the shooter cannot believe his good fortune in having such a gift tossed to him compliments of the management; grateful for every free offer, he rocks back on his heels in surprise and holds out a motionless hand for the present to drop into his palm, but he is so surprised at what is happening he lifts his head to make absolutely sure that his eyes are not deceiving him. Needless to say, the gift, when it comes, misses his outstretched fingertips and drops to the ground.

The shooter should never underestimate the mesmeric qualities of a target that loses speed in this fashion and will do well to remind himself of this whenever he comes up against one that is slowing down at such a seductive rate of knots. Never, never let yourself be lulled into mistakes like this; always get into the habit of actually hardening your resolve when you see a target behaving in this fashion; steel yourself to push a little more weight over that leading foot and finish the gun mount in a crisp, positive style. Only in this way will the muzzles come into the right position to break the target.

Stopping the gun will, of course, result in an incoming quartering bird being missed behind, while lifting the head from the stock will also drag the muzzles high and cause the shot to miss over the top. Let us assume for a moment, though, that you have followed the sequence described earlier and yet the target is still missed. What is wrong? Remember that the barrels are ahead of the target to start with and, as long as the swing was not checked in any shape or form, more often than not the shot will have missed in front. Try moving that hold position a little farther back toward the 'imaginary' fence post and shoot the target a little earlier. Remember, too, what we said about how different shooters will tackle stands their own way, so be careful not to let the man ahead of you dictate where you should break the target. By all means take note of where he shoots it but if you feel more comfortable taking it earlier – or later – then have the courage of your convictions and go for it.

A case in point is an incoming target which is still rising when it comes into shotgun range. The natural temptation is to let it come as close as possible so that you can get a really good look at it as it slows and then starts to drop before moving into the gun mount sequence. In a situation like this it is very easy to follow the example of everybody that goes before, yet you might find it suits your style better to shoot it earlier when it is either still under power or just as it peaks. Watch where other people break it but do not follow on blindly. Get to know your limitations and strong points and make them work for you.

It might be straying from the point a little but a salutary example of how this ability to do your own thing can prove worthwhile shows up reasonably regularly on FITASC Sporting layouts where competitors are rarely restricted by the presence of a safety cage as is the case in English Sporting. Unless the referee actually stipulates (for safety reasons) that a target must be shot in a certain direction, it is left to each shooter to make up his own mind about where it should be broken. Time and time again, though, you will see the first man who shoots at, and misses, say, a fast driven bird in front setting a pattern for

the rest of the squad. They, in turn, face the trap and try and shoot it driven with mixed results, only to kick themselves when some bright spark steps up and asks the referee if it can be shot as a going-away bird instead. He promptly turns his back on the trap, calls for the target and shoots it effortlessly after it has lost all its earlier sting.

Let us return to our incoming dropper. Suppose you have decided, for whatever reason, that you are going to kill it at the point closest to you even though downward descent is greatest and forward momentum is at its lowest. It is certainly worth reminding yourself again about the need to keep that gun mount positive but, before calling for the target, check too that the gun muzzles are under its line of flight so that they come up to the bird, not down on it. The system will work if you let it. Above all, do not be half-

FITASC Sporting shooters are never hampered by having to shoot in a safety cage. This means that they have greater freedom in deciding where they can break the clay.

hearted in your approach: shoot as soon as that stock has been shouldered securely.

Never be tempted to hold too high on this bird's line because to do so will merely increase the chances of it dropping under the barrels before the gun mount has been completed. If this is allowed to happen the target will be lost momentarily from sight and encourage the shooter to commit the two most common mistakes in the book: stopping the swing of the gun and/or lifting his head from the stock as he tries to find the target again.

The need to adopt a below-the-line gun hold is not restricted to targets which show obvious signs of descent as in the case of the incoming dropper. Much more difficult are those which appear to be flying straight and true but which, in fact, have already levelled out and are starting to drop. Targets presented against the depthless backdrop of the sky should always be treated as suspect (especially if the trap is stationed some distance from the shooting position), as too should clays thrown among undulating woodland where the background and tree-line can actually make a dropping target look as if it is rising.

Imperceptible changes in the target's line of flight are more likely to cause difficulties for an inexperienced shooter who addresses the muzzles rigidly to the line of trajectory and then brings the gun through from behind. The bird might well have been flying reasonably level when he first mounted the gun and started to speed up the swing, but, if the target does start to drop and he has not noticed the change, the gun will simply continue along a line which will send the shot harmlessly over the top of the bird. In these situations it is much better to start with the muzzles under its line and let natural eye-to-hand co-ordination bring the muzzles up to the target; that they will also come to the right point ahead of the clay as well is due to nothing more than the legacy of having the gun barrels in front from start to finish.

It cannot be emphasised too strongly that if sportsmen hope to get the most out of Maintained Lead it is best to cultivate a below-the-line gun hold from the outset so that it becomes second nature and an integral part of technique. 'Below-the-line', of course, does not mean holding the muzzles several feet under the path the target will take; a few inches are all that is required to let the eye take in everything about the target and ensure that the hands respond to the signals and so steer the gun into position. In fact, holding too far underneath can be counter-productive: as the gun has now to be lifted quite a long way there is a possibility that the paths of the muzzles and target will cross, causing the shot to go high or forcing the shooter to check the swing and redirect the gun.

There are times, of course, when the Maintained Lead shooter does need to put the muzzles directly on to the line of flight. An obvious candidate is the straight driven clay and one thrown directly overhead from behind where too much lateral deviation will tend to hamper fluent gun-to-target positioning. Others that can also be tackled in this manner include those which are clearly under power and rising at the time the trigger is squeezed, though even here it often pays to bring the gun up, and into, the path of the bird for the reasons just stated. Experience and practice will fine-tune the gun hold position for different targets but until that happy state is reached it is best to steer the middle course and always go for a below-the-line hold on targets which you are not certain about.

Before leaving the subject of incoming droppers, it is worth pointing out that when the clay loses its forward momentum it will normally show a tendency to curl as well as drop. This additional drift is caused by the spin imparted to the target by the trap arm. Again, fight any inclination to counteract the clay's ponderous progress with an equally slow gun mount; force yourself to push your weight over the front foot to minimise the chances of your head lifting off the stock and mount the gun positively to the target when it moves into the area where you plan to break it.

8 In Retreat – Going-Away Clays, Teal and Quartering Birds

It would be quite wrong to say that all clays are broken by a moving gun and forward allowance. There is the very simplest going-away target which leaves a trap concealed at ground level, rises to head height and holds a retreating course long enough for the shooter, if he is so minded, to mount the gun, hold the muzzles stationary and break it by taking deliberate aim. Such obliging targets are rare, but they do exist. And they can be missed – easily.

Going-away targets thrown to represent walked-up game birds are common enough on a Sporting range, but few are ever as simple as the example just quoted. Most, like their real counterparts, rise quickly to beat the gun and will also angle away from danger, thus making it necessary for the shooter to move his gun both up and through to connect with the target. What clays cannot do, unlike the real thing, is swerve or change direction in mid-flight but to compensate for this – and make the shot a little trickier – a course designer will often put the trap off to one side of the competitor to create a wider angle on the bird. This means, of course, that lead of some description is going to have to be imparted if it is to be stopped in its tracks. But let us look at the gentler angles for a moment.

Commonly given advice is to hold the gun low, wait for the target to appear above the barrel, mount the gun and then swing the barrels after it, firing as the muzzles come up, and through, the bird. If it is also going off to one side, the gun must be swung along from behind and accelerated out in front to create the necessary forward allowance. A great many people sincerely believe that the only way to shoot going-away birds which show any tendency to lift or quarter from the shooting station is by bringing the gun from behind and firing as the speeding muzzles pass the target's leading edge. They are welcome to their views of course. But after coaching not a few rank beginners and straightening out a similar number of experienced sportsmen I have come to the conclusion that such dogma is both off beam and somewhat limiting to people who might find it more rewarding to use Maintained Lead.

My reasons for saying this are twofold: first, and most important, a lot of so-called simple going-away targets are missed because the man on the trigger slows down when his gun closes up on the bird and, second, others seem unable to move the gun fast enough through the target to get the shot string out in front.

Both have fairly serious repercussions on marksmanship, but of the two, it is the first that gives most concern because, if an otherwise intelligent human being can slow up on such mild-angled targets as this, he can – and will – show similar inclinations on other birds too. Nobody has yet been able to explain why it should happen, but it does. People (and not just novices either) can string together a long run of misses because they will insist on shooting at the target rather than in front of it. It is a fatal attraction that can prove well nigh impossible to break clear of.

John has set himself to shoot a going-away bird which will quarter across his front. It is coming from a trap concealed behind the bush and below feet level. His weight is well forward (to stop him shooting high) and his left foot points to his pre-selected killing point. The gun barrel addresses a mark midway between this and the edge of the bush where he will first see the emerging clay.

The only explanation I can give for it is that the eye is coping very nicely thank you watching the bird and feeding in all the right information when all of a sudden the blurred gun barrel hoves into sight, distracting the eye and impairing the concentration. The mind, momentarily unable to cope with this intrusion, reacts in predictable fashion by trying to divide its attention between the target and the indistinct line of the gun rib. And our subconscious, in true cluttered fashion, decides that a compromise is called for here and since the two are fairly evenly aligned, agrees that it is in everybody's best interests just to pull the trigger and see what happens. The all-time loser, of course, is speed of swing.

This amounts to a disastrous upset in a method which relies on barrel speed to break targets but until the brain learns to disregard the intrusion it is something which will, unfortunately, crop up time and time again unless the shooter manages to master this particular instance of mind over matter. This is no easy task unless the shooter already has a clear picture in his mind of the relationship that must exist between the barrel and the target before the trigger is squeezed. Maintained Lead might not be the cure for all ills but what it does do is instill a very clear barrel-to-target picture that overrides uncertainty and gives the brain a yardstick by which to work.

With this method the eyes do all the work and direct the barrels into position ahead of the target without their encroaching on and influencing the eye-to-target relationship. By the time the rib comes into peripheral vision the gun mount has all but been completed and all that remains is for the trigger to be squeezed. The only way the swing can now be slowed or stopped is for the eyes to pull away from the target completely and focus, instead, on the mounted gun. It would be foolish to say that this cannot happen because nobody can legislate for the human mind. However, the probability of such an aberration happening is much more remote, espe-cially if the sportsman gets into the habit of firing almost as soon as the gun stock is securely mounted into the face and shoulder.

The problem of a swing which is too slow to overhaul even a shallow quartering target is something that is best left to the individual to sort out, but if glucose tablets and a good night's sleep cannot cure such sluggishness, he might as well admit defeat and start his gun barrels where he means them to end up – out in front of the bird. This serves a dual purpose: firstly it puts the gunner in with a better than even chance of placing the string in front of the target and, secondly, it helps him develop a mental picture that will stand him in good stead on every other target which needs forward allowance – namely, that the gun muzzles must be in front of the clay when the gun is fired. This might sound a little too obvious at the first time of reading but a great many shooters do not truly understand the picture they are trying to create; if they did, their barrels would never slow up in the way they do when the two come together. Once a shooter gets into the habit of seeing a gap between the muzzles and the target he will find himself well on the way to overcoming the problem and will need only to work on his foot and gun position to steer the barrels into the right place for each shot.

It needs to be repeated that as few targets ever fly absolutely true from the stand the shooter must always treat a bird which appears to be going straight with extreme caution and be sure in his own mind that he knows what it is doing. Regulation trap layouts are chosen with high visibility in mind; in other words, they are built with a background which allows the competitor to see the target as soon as it clears the trap house roof. This enables him to make fast, accurate assessments of speed and angles and take the necessary action with the gun.

The Sporting shooter, though, will rarely be so lucky with the background: trees, banks, bushes, hollows and hills could well conspire to hide the truth about the bird's trajectory and seriously disadvantage anybody who has not been paying attention. The same is also true of its rate of climb; these very same natural features can combine to make a bird look as if it is rising when, in fact, it is holding a fairly flat trajectory. It should be noted too that the backdrop, equally, can camouflage the steepness of its actual ascent. In these situations no shooting method yet devised will compensate for a misread target.

The most common question asked by people undecided about Maintained Lead is how it can possibly be of use against birds which come out of the trap flat and take an arrow-straight course away from the shooting position. The short answer is that it is of no use: the angle between where it is first seen and then broken is so narrow as to make Follow-Through – as well as Maintained Lead – redundant. With a bird that rises to eye level and stays there, it is sufficient for the gun to be mounted and the shot fired. Provided the shooter keeps his eyes on the target and his head on the stock, it will be hit. But, to repeat the question, how many are ever as obliging as this? Once the target's rate of climb and/or sideways angle increases, Maintained Lead becomes an ever more effective way of dealing with it.

This is not to say that if a shooter is perfectly happy and successful in coming from behind the target he should change. Heaven forbid the thought! If you have got something that works for you, stick with it. As we stated earlier, it is not our intention to try to effect change for change's sake, but merely to show people who experience problems with a particular target or targets that maybe they will come up with an answer or two by keeping an open mind on why they miss. If 'keeping an open mind' means giving Maintained Lead a meaningful trial then why not? If you cannot hit them consistently with Follow-Through, you have everything to gain and nothing to lose!

The high gun hold favoured by some Down-the-Line trap shooters is a form of Maintained Lead. They start to move as soon as the rising and quartering target appears under the barrel.

If you still do not believe that maintaining the lead on going-away targets can work, try to find time to go and watch some top-class Down-the-Line trap shooters in action next time they are in your area. Certainly, a great many will mount their guns on the top of the trap house sixteen yards in front and wait until the clay has appeared and started to climb away before they move their gun quickly after, and up to it before pulling the trigger. They will also pull through the angled birds and fire as the gun muzzle passes its leading edge to give it forward allowance. But keep an eye open as well for those competitors who address the mounted gun to a point of thin air two or three feet above the trap. They are using a form of Maintained Lead. Instead of looking for the emerging target over the top of the rib they are now getting their first sight of the clay under the barrels and, when it appears, simply moving the gun into the line of the rising bird.

The same action is taken by a Sporting shooter who uses Maintained Lead; the only difference now is that he calls for the bird with an unmounted gun, rather than one already bedded securely into the shoulder pocket and cheek pouch. The Sporting shot, in fact, has got an important advantage over the other because he, at least, knows where the target is going, unlike our trap-shooting cousin who stands behind a machine which moves constantly to change the angle of the next target out. We can use this knowledge to full advantage by picturing where, on the flight path, we want to break it and where we will get a first, clear view of it after it leaves the trap. Once these two reference points have been noted the muzzles can be addressed to the mid-point before we look back for the target. As soon as it appears in proper focus the eyes stay glued to it and the gun is moved, mounted and then shot; in this way, the barrels stay ahead of the target and will be directed into position by eye-to-hand coordination.

Whether you use Follow-Through or Maintained Lead is immaterial when it comes to countering the most common reason for missing a target of this kind: head lifting. It is imperative here to make sure that the face comes to rest on the gun stock and stays there until after the shot has been taken. In some people the temptation to lift the head just before the gun has been mounted is strong indeed. But the temptation to watch the target in this fashion must be resisted at all costs because moving the head will simply drag the barrels off line and will also contribute to an overly lazy, pokey swing which cancels out all that earlier effort. The surest way of nipping this fault in the bud is to think about weight distribution before the target is called and push more weight over that leading leg to make sure the head goes into a forward position where it will contact the gun stock and stay there.

When it comes to targets which quarter away, the simple technique we have just used to handle one going up and away remains the same, only now we must give some attention to the role our feet and gun position are going to play in putting the barrel the right distance ahead of the bird. Here, we are not dealing with a going-away clay which drifts slightly off a straight line, but one which shows a definite edge to it: the sort that, if it were a fleeing game bird, would be showing the shooter part of its head and some flank as well as it tries to make it to safety.

Decide where you will see the target properly and create a picture in your mind of where it will be broken. Remember what we said in an earlier section about gun swing and how it can slow down if the front foot is incorrectly positioned? Make use of it! Even though retreating quartering targets of this sort do not have particularly fierce angles to them, they still demand that the gun should move without the slightest interruption, so point that front foot in the direction of where the target is going to be struck and, to make sure there is extra swing on hand if needed, turn those toes a little bit further along the path it is going to take. All that remains now is to hold the muzzles to the mid-point, look

Ready: *this quartering going-away clay has been thrown from a trap to the left of, and behind, the shooting position. Note how the barrels are out in front and under the line of the bird already.*

Move: *John has now seen this fast-moving clay clearly and is starting to move the barrels to stay ahead of it.*

Mount: *by moving the gun smoothly and letting his eyes read the target John has managed to maintain the necessary lead . . .*

. . . and without further delay he squeezes the trigger.

The gun swing is maintained and, in the same split second, the target is turned into a satisfying heap of dust.

back for the bird and check that our weight is nicely over the front leg before calling 'Pull'. Again, as soon as the bird is in clear view, Move, Mount and Shoot.

Most people who bring the gun from behind a clay prefer to hold the muzzles to the line so that when the clay becomes airborne they merely have to move in a line which allows them to sweep straight through the target. This is an integral part of the method in use and, provided the gun moves at the right speed, will work very well. However, for Maintained Lead, it is better to hold the unmounted gun muzzles fractionally under the expected trajectory and bring the moving gun up and into the path of the target. This, as already explained in Chapter 7 is because

the hand and eye find it easier to bring the barrels up to a mark rather than down on it, and also because the sportsman can keep the bird in view throughout.

Also falling very firmly into the going-away category is the Springing Teal target, a bird that causes untold problems even for very accomplished performers. It is a target which can come in all shapes and forms – from one that is thrown at near-supersonic speeds climbing to a great height in next to no time, to another which is merely lobbed into space, rising only a few yards before dropping back to ground. More often than not the shooter will be positioned behind the trap house but it is not all that uncommon to find the stand placed out to one side; this

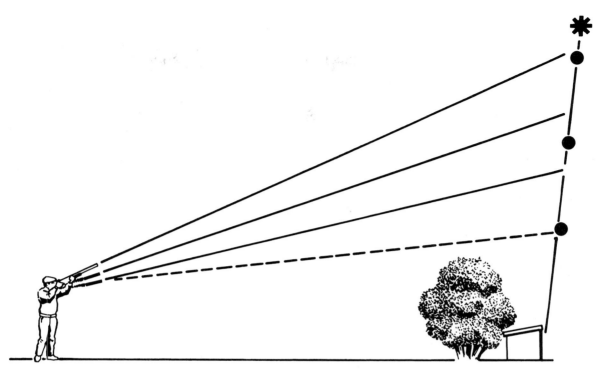

Don't try to shoot Teal too quickly – pick a point where you will see the target clearly. Decide where you plan to break it and let the gun barrels address the mid-point. Move and Mount as soon as the target comes into proper focus.

creates something of an edge-on target which now needs vertical lead and a certain amount of lateral movement to the gun as well to bring about a successful shot. But whatever the angle encountered here the unbreakable rule is to base your approach on the target's speed. In other words, always adopt a Ready position based on where the target is going to be seen properly after it has left the trap. Never try to mount the gun when the clay is still a blur. To do so will merely make things harder than they really are.

Firstly, make up your mind about where you will find the clay in nice, sharp relief and then decide where you would like to break it. Having made a mental picture of these two reference points, address the muzzles to the mid-point and look past the gun for the target. As soon as it comes into view, move the gun, mount and shoot when the butt reaches the face and shoulder. Do not worry

if you lose sight of the clay under the barrels just as the gun has been mounted – providing you have concentrated hard on the bird throughout its flight and mounted the gun smoothly, the barrels will be in the right position anyway. Remember: Move, Mount, Shoot. Do not be tempted to hang on to the swing too long before squeezing the trigger as this will only encourage you to start looking for the target and increase the risk of the gun slowing down. It also creates an ideal opportunity for the head to lift off the stock.

From the outset always strive to cultivate a silky smooth mount on birds of this sort and do not allow yourself to dip the barrels by mounting the stock first. If this does happen it is usually a sure sign that the swing has slowed or stopped altogether, allowing the target to close the gap or even overtake the gun. Either way, such a ragged gun mount as this will do nothing but hamper quick and positive acquisition of the climbing target. Practice makes perfect, of course, and it might take a practice shot or two just to become accustomed to it, but once you have got used to losing temporary sight of the target your confidence will grow apace and the rewards will follow.

If you should misread the speed of the target and find that it is above the barrel just as the gun is being mounted, there is no other option but to hang fire a moment or two and push the muzzles up, and through, and pull the trigger as they pass the bird. What you should not do is try to retrieve the situation by giving such a rising bird 'automatic' forward allowance by lifting your head off the stock, aiming at the bird and remaining ever hopeful that the barrel will be ramped sufficiently to send the shot charge above it in prescribed fashion.

The trouble with this slightly scientific poke and hope method is that it does work some of the time on mild climbers and might even persuade a lazy shooter to believe that he has found a variant that is worth working on. The drawback, of course, is that the position of the eye above the rib is ultra-critical to its effectiveness and can give rise to terrible inconsistencies. It is also habit forming, so if anybody finds themselves lapsing into sloppy ways they should act positively and stop it before things get out of hand. The only answer to a bird which catches the shooter out by rising faster than expected is to take the next shot by putting the muzzles a little higher on the hold position, thus giving him a little more time to see the bird and move the gun.

Much the same approach should be applied to a teal bird viewed from the side but, as few ever travel on a true vertical path, the shooter now at least is unlikely to lose sight of the target when the gun is mounted. This makes matters easier, but only fractionally. The biggest problem here is in making sure that the eyes remain glued to the thin, edge-on profile of the clay and ensuring that they are not transferred, even briefly, to the rib to check its position against that of the target. Make sure too that if the target is taking a path away from the vertical the foot position allows those arms to move the gun beyond the point where it will be broken.

It is invariably easier to hit a teal target on the way up or very nearly at the peak of its flight than when it is dropping. However, if you find that you must shoot it on the way down (it could be that a helpful breeze pushes it back toward the shooting position), get those barrels well underneath, watch the target and keep the gun moving as the trigger is touched off. Some lucky souls actually find it easier to hit birds which are dropping but, unless you happen to find that you are one of them, stick to shooting them on the up. You will not be too disappointed with the results.

9 Rabbits

So far we have concentrated on how best we can tackle airborne targets or, rather, targets thrown above eye level. There is a good reason for this: English Sporting rules limit the use of non-standard (110mm) clays to 10 per cent of a shoot's total so it follows that most of the targets encountered during a 'typical' shooting day will, likely as not, be thrown to represent the kind of free-flying quarry species found in the field proper. This means showing them above head height. The 10 per cent rule also takes in other special targets by way of minis, midis and battues but these, like 110mm clays, are normally presented with some height to them so they can, for the time being at least, be put into the same sort of category. This, then, leaves us with the rabbit.

In many respects the rabbit does not deserve to have 'special' status conferred on him by the people who lay down the rules. Of all the quarry species in Britain the humble bunny is one that, with the wood-pigeon, forms the backbone of sport for many people who take their gun into the countryside. In some areas rabbit populations have reached pre-myxomatosis levels which actually reverses the rabbit's 'special' status – by being shot at nine times in ten rather than once in a blue moon!

Despite this, the fact remains that of all the specials (with the possible exception of battues) the inanimate rabbit clay is a target on which far too many people can come unstuck. Poor technique is usually to blame, but how can sportsmen hope to improve when they do not get enough practice at them to start with? The situation is somewhat better in the world of FITASC Sporting where no rule exists on the number of so-called specials that a shoot must limit itself

to. In fact, the reverse is often the case here, so much so that it is not unusual to encounter 25-bird layouts that have upwards of half a dozen bunnies bouncing around at all sorts of different angles, speeds and distances. Anybody, then, who nurses an ambition to move into the much more demanding world of international Sporting would be well advised to search out those English Sporting grounds which do throw rabbit targets and brush up on their technique in readiness for what lies ahead. It will be time well spent.

Sportsmen revel in the enormous variety of targets given them on a Sporting range. It is the chief reason why this particular branch of the sport has become the most popular form of clay shooting in Britain. And judging by the number of other countries now turning away from the rigidly disciplined trap and skeet events, it is a sport which, more and more, is gaining universal appeal.

While it takes a very special kind of aptitude and application to break 100 straight at these other highly regimented disciplines it must be said that an even greater depth of all-round skill has to be developed by anybody who wants to shoot Sporting to the best of his abilities. This is because each ground is free to use whatever target speeds and angles it cares to, unlike the rather narrow confines of regulation trap and skeet layouts where angles and speeds are rigidly (and uniformly) controlled. No such limitations exist on a Sporting range. If any do crop up then it is due either to a lack of imagination on the part of the man who sets up the course or to the topography of his ground: but give the right man enough woodland, open ground, hills and hollows on which to station his traps and the shooter will be treated to a veritable feast of variety.

A trapper's view of the action on a rabbit layout. The shooting ground has laid a rubber mat to help the target off to a smooth start. The clay will appear as a crosser to the waiting gun who must kill it between the two wood pallets.

Unfortunately, few grounds in overcrowded Britain run to such lavish possibilities. A great many clubs and private grounds are limited to an acreage which may, or may not, contain some of the features that go to make a thoroughly interesting course. Some, it is true, are so strapped for space that they are positively pedestrian in the targets they throw; angles and speeds show little, if any, variation from one meeting to another because trap positions have been fixed to meet the wishes of local councils and nearby householders who want the noise of gunfire to go in the opposite direction.

But the saving grace in all this is that no two Sporting grounds are ever the same and such is the popularity of English Sporting that its followers rarely have to travel far to find a fresh ground and fresh targets. By using two, three or, hopefully, more grounds a shotgunner will fill in the gaps which will surely exist should he decide to restrict his activities to one venue.

Even if you do not harbour dreams of taking part in the highly charged atmosphere of a big 150- or 200-bird FITASC championship and simply want to content yourself with English Sporting, it will still pay to search out a rabbit stand or two. Somewhere on your travels you are bound to come across this target and will need to shoot it well to put in a high score, maybe to take a class prize, hopefully to win the shoot outright. Your chances of doing this will get progressively harder, though, if you habitually struggle to hit them.

Too many people, sadly, talk themselves out of hitting even the most straightforward rabbit. They fret about where they should try to break it and worry themselves to a near standstill over the possibility that it might hit a bump and bounce high just as they squeeze the trigger. If 'rabbits' had half an idea about how they petrified some humans they would never again worry about being hunted by them! Yet shooters do allow themselves to slip into a trance-like state when confronted by a clay which behaves like no other by bouncing quickly across the grass. Worse, they allow themselves to take on board a number of bad habits which, they convince themselves, will break the 'spell' and hopefully put shot and rabbit on a collision course. Such trickery rarely works of course. But the people suffering from a really bad case of rabbit-itis are those who turn to their friends just before they go up to shoot and make the comment that they have always struggled on rabbits and that the gallery should not expect great things this time around. Such a defeatist attitude really does give the advantage to the clay.

First, last and always these targets demand confidence and this means having utter faith in the very same technique (with minor adjust-

This rabbit was missed. The hunched shoulders and neck suggest that restricted gun mount and swing were responsible.

ments) which has already served so well on the tower birds and crossers we have just tackled.

So what are the difficulties? Heading the list is incorrect gun hold before the target is called for, with a contorted, and unnatural, stance coming a close second. Nobody would ever say that rabbits are easy things to hit but, by the same token, it has to be said that the two problems outlined here occur because the shooter is not thinking about the target and allows himself to believe that any gun hold – provided it is below eye level – will be near enough as to make no earthly difference to the success of his shot. Would that were true! Too many of these targets are missed for no other reason than that the shooter held too high and too far back on its line of flight.

If we are to deal effectively with rabbits, the gun muzzles must always assume a position which puts them on the target's line at

the start of the Move, Mount, Shoot sequence. If the muzzles can be held slightly under this line when the target appears then so much the better because now the shooter is in far greater control and can bring his gun into the clay. But let us stay with initial gun position for a moment and look at the problems that can be encountered by holding too high. For the time being we will assume we are shooting at a quickish crossing target 30 yards in front.

Holding high means that when the target does appear it will scurry out underneath the gun and force the luckless shooter to chop down on it just before he pulls the trigger, a movement which all too often leads to him shooting low into the ground or poking the gun and missing behind. It is a bad habit which, on its own, is enough to foster inconsistency. But let us not forget the man who holds the gun too far back on the line of flight as well; now we have steered ourselves

Even champions miss from time to time! John has just shot a low going-away bird and did not readjust his stance for the rabbit on report. He is too upright and the second shot has gone high.

into a situation where the gun must be moved very quickly indeed to catch and then overtake the target before the trigger finger can go to work. On their own, each of these two extremely common faults can easily result in a missed target but, put them both together, and the chances of the rabbit making it safely back to 'burrow' are doubled. The combination of a downward gun movement and an over-fast swing leaves precious little leeway should the target decide to put in an unscheduled jump just as the shooter lights the blue touch-paper.

It should not be forgotten either that groundsmen are also fond of erecting barriers in the form of bales or logs along the rabbit's path where, once reached, it is classed as lost. Usually shooting grounds play fair by putting such barriers in a place where the shooter can get off a reasonably settled first shot. But if you are in competition do not always bank on it. I have seen enough rabbit

layouts in my time to come to the conclusion that some groundsmen have thoroughly evil intentions and, given the chance, will take the rabbits' trick of dashing across a narrow woodland rise (thus demanding a snap shot at close range) a little too far. You no sooner see the target and mount the gun than it reaches the barrier and is lost.

Such fleeting clays can cause enough trouble for a Maintained Lead shooter, but this pales into insignificance beside an inexperienced performer who relies on coming fast from behind and using barrel speed to produce the right forward allowance. By the time such a shooter has reacted to this fast, nimble target and got his barrels moving the rabbit will be well across the gap and heading for safety just as the mounted gun is being thrown headlong after it. The shot that follows amounts to little more than a token gesture and is usually yards behind to boot.

These targets are a severe enough test for

any sportsman but, by starting with the barrel ahead of the rabbit, a shooter gains valuable space and will increase his chances of hitting it with a gun mount and swing which are both positive and controlled. However, not all rabbits are such speed merchants of course. More often than not a competitor will be given plenty of time to see the target clearly and shoot before it either disappears behind a screen or stops rolling. But pace – or lack of it – is immaterial. What matters most is technique.

If you do not feel confident shooting rabbit targets it is easy to be persuaded that a slightly altered stance and swing are all that is needed to start hitting the clay consistently – how else can the sight of people crouching, stooping and twisting be explained. Yet the same basic technique that is used for other targets is the one which should be applied here. In other words, the front foot should be put in a position which allows the gun to be moved freely once the stock comes into the face and shoulder, and the muzzles left 'on hold' midway between the place the rabbit will be seen clearly and then broken. Note the word 'clearly': if the rabbit is a particularly fast one it will, if the shooter looks too far back, merely appear as a blur across his

vision, tempting him to 'jump' the gun which causes the barrels to move too soon and lead to a probable miss in front.

It has to be said as well that this is the point at which people who do struggle show a lemming-like tendency to seal their fate good and proper. All too clearly they realise that to keep the barrels moving with the line of the target they must ensure that the gun is held low and so reduce any possibility of the barrel riding high during the mount and, thus, causing a miss over the top. The encouraging thing here is that the shooters, at least, do have some idea of the problems caused by a target appearing at floor level. Unfortunately they then hamper their chances by applying some muddled thinking to the equation, sacrificing an unchecked swing by bending their knees into a grotesque crouch and/or adopting an exaggerated forward stoop by pushing their head and shoulders as far forward as they dare without toppling over.

Keeping the weight forward does keep the head on a mounted gun stock, but adopting an outlandish forward tilt is not the answer. The simplest and neatest way to achieve free lateral movement while keeping the head in contact with the wood throughout the Mount

The only way to keep the head on the stock is to bend from the waist and push more weight over that leading leg.

and Shoot sequence is to shift more weight over the leading leg and bring the barrels down to the target by bending from the waist. As long as the weight remains over the front foot the head will automatically go into the stock and stay put throughout the shot while the weight distribution will cancel out any tendency to straighten the body and so pull off the line of the target.

Crouched stances should be avoided at all costs. However, the shooter must also be on his guard not to go too far the other way and adopt an overly upright stance with his hands held low against his body to create the essential muzzle-to-target relationship. To do so will cause the gun to come above the rabbit when the stock is mounted, resulting in a miss which, while proving no danger to the rabbit, would fell anything flying three or four feet off the ground.

Some clubs and ground owners (and a lot of sportsmen for that matter!) do not like rabbits because they can, on uneven ground, act in a decidedly inconsistent manner; every so often one will hit a bump and bounce off the ground in a quite spectacular fashion just as the shooter has committed himself to squeezing the trigger. In such situations the aggrieved party can complain, with some justification, that the target is unfair but, for all that, the extra fun rabbits bring to a shoot is well worth the occasional upset. There is, of course, no possibile excuse for a course organiser using a runway that encourages such targets to leave the ground at every opportunity. Every attempt must be made before a shoot starts to iron out obvious trouble spots on the runway so that each rabbit travels as true as possible and gives each competitor a fair challenge.

Some people are better at overcoming sudden changes in the flight of a rabbit than others. But one small advantage in using Maintained Lead is that by keeping the gun in front a shooter is better able to watch the target and make minor adjustments should the clay do something untoward just as it comes into the killing area. It really is bad luck if the rabbit bounces just as the trigger is squeezed (whatever method is being used) but, by keeping the gun low and ahead of the target, the Maintained Lead shooter does retain an element of control for an accurate second shot – an advantage which is not always on offer to the man who holds too high and races through the target at too great a speed.

Some grounds, commendably, try to make targets as scrupulously even and fair for everybody by going to the trouble and expense of building special trackways with a surface of graded sand and ash. But any short cropped grass track free of irregularities will suffice. Dusty surfaces, though, do help shooters pin-point where they missed the target thanks to a convenient dust cloud being thrown up by the passing shot column. Do not, however, read too much into what you think you see. It is not unusual to find a shooter shaking his head in bewilderment after seemingly surrounding the target with pellets. They will have kicked up a huge cloud of dust all around the target yet the rabbit bowls out unharmed the other side and continues merrily on its way. In these situations it is easy to believe that a patchy pattern (or an armour-plated target!) is responsible for letting the target pass through untouched. But the likeliest cause is a miss in front: the swarming pellets create a dust storm just ahead of the clay which, a split second later, finds itself in the midst of the commotion, thus creating the impression that the pellets were on line.

This illusion is more common than people think and is particularly prevalent in the case of targets which quarter away from the shooting position. The angle between a miss in front and one behind is extremely narrow, and the target passes into the dust cloud almost instantaneously Regardless of the shooting style used, the danger now is that the beguiled shooter is tempted to increase his lead rather than reduce it so it goes without saying that some care and not a little thought should be exercised before rushing

This target has been thrown as a quartering driven rabbit. The position of the gun barrels throughout the sequence tells its own story.

into a remedy that, in the end, might prove doubly wrong.

Quartering targets too have gained a reputation for being impervious to the shot pattern sometimes with justification. The trouble here is that a number of target manufacturers produce clays that, by necessity, have to be made tougher than usual to withstand the powerful throwing action of automatic traps. If they were too soft there would be an unsatisfactory increase in the number which break on release. But occasionally batches are made which are far stronger than necessary, so strong that several pellets can hit the target and pass straight through without stopping it in its tracks. A careful inspection of targets at the end of the shoot might sometimes help confirm earlier suspicions that the batch in use was suspect, especially if more than a reasonable number are lying unbroken but neatly punched and drilled like a colander. As a matter of interest,

the most holes I have seen in an unbroken rabbit clay were seven – evidence enough, surely, for the shooting ground to have had the entire batch replaced free of charge by the manufacturer!

Even properly mixed rabbit clays can withstand a direct blow from a pellet, especially if it strikes the thick rolling edge of a target thrown away from the shooter. It is doubtful that a rabbit caught in the centre of the pattern would ever escape intact but it might get away with it should it merely be clipped by a weakened pellet travelling along on the edge of the pattern. In these situations it is best to put aside those skeet shells loaded with small shot and plump instead for a good-quality trap load carrying 7's. Not only will the slightly tighter pattern put more pellets on target but those that do find the mark will hit it with greater energy and stop it in thoroughly convincing fashion.

Skeet cartridges are perfectly adequate for

This quartering-away rabbit is already halfway home and the swing-from-behind shooter has not yet overhauled it with his barrels. The further it goes the harder it will be to break.

close-range work where a wider pattern carries a marginal advantage but, as the range increases, the only really reliable choice is a trap shell. If you are confident in the way that hard-nickel-coated pellets perform then by all means use them against edge-on going-away targets. Such full-energy pellets can give the clay a belt up the backside from which it will never recover but be careful when the target is presented as a long-range crosser. It is now possible that one or two pellets will punch a neat hole without breaking the clay whereas the same number of lead pellets which flatten on impact could crack it.

Do not be overawed by the speed of the rabbit target. Strange as it may sound, this turn of speed can often work to a shooter's advantage because he is not able to dwell on his swing and mount. He merely sees the target, moves the gun and when the stock comes into his face and shoulder he fires;

eye-to-hand co-ordination ensures that the barrel is pointing in the right direction when the shot leaves the barrel. Another advantage to speed is that a fast-moving target pitches itself headlong into the shot string as well, thus increasing the chances of it being struck by a number of pellets.

Compare this, if you will, with 'rolling rabbits' – clays that instead of being thrown full tilt from a powered trap are simply placed on a wooden ramp and trundled across the ground at a pace that might just overhaul an athletic tortoise. These can prove more awkward to hit than one with an open throttle so do not be lulled into thinking that they are easy! The temptations are many. The first is to shoot directly at one with a moving gun and trust that the speed of swing is not too great to throw the shot charge too far out in front. Its slow speed also encourages people to mount the gun too soon and deliberately aim at a spot in front and trust that the shot

A nice forward lean but hasn't this competitor forgotten something? His head is off the stock and the shot will surely go high if he does not correct the fault before he pulls the trigger.

will intercept it. The most consistent way, though, is to keep the gun low, hold it ahead of the target and ensure that the weight is over the front foot to keep head and face on the stock. Pick a spot in front of the rabbit and Move, Mount, Shoot by matching the speed of the barrels to that of this infuriatingly slow target.

Another frustrating angle can be the rabbit thrown downhill. Again, this might be a crossing target, straight going-away, quarterer or incomer. But regardless of where it is going or coming from, the shooter need only keep his technique simple to ensure that he breaks more than his fair share. As long as the gun is held under the line, the gun will come up into position every time and require nothing more on the shooter's part than to pull the trigger and release the shot.

10 Special Problems – Battues, Midis, Minis and Rockets

BATTUES

Recently I asked a fellow shooting instructor whether he could put a finger on the targets which caused his clients the most aggravation. The reply was immediate and illuminating: 'Rabbits and battues. No doubt about it.'

I have no evidence from other instructors to support this statement but as these two figure high on my own list I would not be very surprised to hear that other coaches, too, find themselves being kept busy on the same targets. This is because battues, like the rabbits we discussed earlier, are classed as special targets and thus restricted in number. In other words, people get too little opportunity to sharpen their technique on this spectacular target; so much so that on the few occasions they do tangle with it, the battue very often comes out on top. It is no wonder, then, that there is a regular trade back at the shooting school.

The situation would not be quite so bad if clubs – unencumbered as they are by rules which restrict this target in registered competitions – were to liven up their layouts by throwing a lot more battues than they do already at regular practice sessions and non-registered competitions. If they were to do this, a great many difficulties would, I am certain, quickly disappear.

Unfortunately, clubs, for whatever reason, do seem rather reluctant to put right the shortfall and outwardly appear to be quite happy existing on a regular (though somewhat tedious) diet of standard-size targets. I

have no idea why this should be. Maybe they are put off by the small extra cost of buying battues as opposed to 110mm clays, or maybe they think that special new traps will have to be bought out of club funds to throw them. Neither excuse holds water. The slight extra cost (and it is slight) can easily be justified in the extra enjoyment they bring the shooter, and (as we explain in Chapter 13) existing hand-operated traps are all any club needs to show battues to their best advantage. So why the seeming reluctance? All I can think is that an undeserved aura of mystery has grown up around the battue to such an extent that clubs unthinkingly steer clear of it. This is a terrible pity really because, of all the targets at a club's disposal, the battue and its fast-flying characteristics is the one which can help transform proceedings.

Until more use is made of this clay, people will continue to struggle. But, strange as it may seem, the battue is not as difficult to break as its reputation might suggest, though it is not hard to see how it has managed to acquire its status. If you have not yet encountered battues, think of a standard target from a trap, replace it with a wafer-thin clay of the same diameter . . . and watch the speed near enough double thanks to a slim profile which helps it slice through the air better than its plump cousin and carry much, much farther. It carries so well, in fact, that when a standard clay has lost its initial speed and started to drift lazily to earth a battue from the same trap will likely as not still be going strong and, because it lacks the other's

The wafer-thin profile of the battue (left) as compared with the rocket (centre) and rabbit means that it can fly very quickly.

deep skirt, when it does slow down it rolls on its side and plummets downward in a wide, spectacular arc.

Unless the battue is thrown as a straight-driven bird (where it will normally be shown full view) a course designer might well throw it as a high, wide crosser and engineer things so that the bird initially appears edge-on to the shooting position but then rolls sideways to expose its full surface area before arcing to ground. This turn of speed and rolling flight characteristic is the reason it proves such an awkward proposition to so many people. Yet they are not as difficult as they first seem, provided they are tackled with a sound technique. Let us start by looking at straight-driven battues.

The only real difference between these and the normal-size targets we have already tackled will be speed, so the first adjustment that needs to be made is that of gun hold. The trap most people fall into is under-

estimating the target's speed and holding the muzzles too close to the point where they first see the clay. This leads to the target getting past the barrels before they can react to it and means, of course, that they must now come from behind very quickly to overtake the target and get in front before a shot can be fired. If you feel happiest coming from behind in this manner and you hit the target consistently, by all means stick with it but if you start to miss more than you break, be prepared to change.

When it comes to very fast battues you stand a far better chance of hitting them by using Maintained Lead rather than trying, vainly, to sweep after, then through, the fast approaching target. In some circumstances this is a well nigh impossible proposition anyway, particularly if there is very little space between seeing the bird clearly and its disappearing overhead. The faster the target covers the distance, the harder it becomes to

Don't be frightened by the speed and curving flight of a wafer-thin battue. The golden rule is to choose your hold position carefully and to bring the gun into the path of the clay. Squeeze the trigger as soon as the stock has been securely mounted.

pull through from behind. It is tempting to think that all that is required is a faster gun mount and faster swing, but this would be a mistake – such action might work for an experienced performer but for the rest more speed almost always equals less gun control and wild, wild shooting.

Maintained Lead, on the other hand, offers a practical solution to the problem of having too little time on this kind of target because, by putting the barrels out in front to start with, a sportsman is better able to move his gun, mount and shoot without undue rush. Remember that the procedure for breaking a straight tower battue differs little from any other driven target, so determine where you will see it clearly and where you plan to break it before placing the gun muzzles midway between the two. Now look back to its entry point and, as soon as the target appears, start to move the gun. Devote all your atten-

tion to the bird. Your hands will direct the gun into position so do not worry about the lead needed to break it. This takes care of itself, leaving you free to squeeze the trigger as soon as the butt has been mounted securely. If the target appears slightly blurred when you first see it, try shifting your gaze a little farther out along its path and adjust your gun hold accordingly. If you are not seeing it properly then you are looking too close to the trap and there will be a tendency to move too soon, with the probable consequence of a miss in front.

There is often a temptation on fast, difficult targets like this to 'hold fire' for a moment or two to check quickly that the barrel-to-target alignment looks right before the trigger is squeezed, but it is a temptation which should be avoided wherever possible. It is worth repeating that consciously shifting the gaze from target to barrel will alter the area of

111

focus and cause the swing of the gun to slow down or, in really bad cases, to stop altogether. It also opens the door to that other terrible habit – head lifting. No matter how unsure you are about the target it is best to put your trust in eye/hand co-ordination and fire as soon as the gun has been mounted properly. It will rarely fail.

If the speed of the target gives enough time for you to shoot it in front, put your weight over the leading leg and set about it in the manner described but always be ready to transfer to the back foot if the bird only offers a chance directly overhead. Time spent practising gun mounting from the back leg will never be wasted and it will repay itself time and time again on driven targets of all types where extra gun movement is needed to deliver unhindered forward allowance up to, and beyond, the perpendicular.

Battues can be thrown at a variety of angles but the most commonly encountered is probably the crossing battue which is placed upside-down on the trap arm. By putting it the wrong way like this a shoot organiser can now get a target which zips out on edge to the shooter before it loses a little bit of momentum and rolls sideways, momentarily exposing its full surface area to the waiting gun. Unfortunately, the fact that it has shown itself so obligingly is merely the signal that it is losing forward power and is starting to slice downward, thus compounding the problems of trying to smash it. Not only does this one need the right amount of forward allowance, it also demands that the gun is under the target as well when the shot is fired to take care of its descent which, after rolling over, gets ever steeper in a very short space of time. If there is a secret to hitting this target

English and British FITASC Grand Prix champion Mick Rouse shows how to tackle a fast, driven battue passing slightly left to right. His gun is held well out from the trap (hidden by the ridge) and he is looking back for the clay.

consistently it is in timing the shot to coincide with the target rolling on its side. If the shot can be made just as it flips over, the need to get underneath as well will be marginally less than is the case a second or two later when the angle of descent will be very much greater.

Whereas an overhead driven battue is seen full view after it has left the trap, the crossing version will, likely as not, be showing nothing more than its pencil-thin outline so be extra careful in deciding where you look for it. The killing point, of course, takes care of itself so build your stance around this and move the gun barrels back along the line of flight. It might help here to shuffle the feet a little further round just in case you have under-estimated its speed and need to swing farther than anticipated. Hopefully you will have judged it correctly at the first time of asking but it never hurts to put aside a little extra insurance as far as free gun movement is concerned. Remember, too, that the bird will be starting to drop when it turns so put the muzzles of the unmounted gun under the line of the target and bring the barrels up, and into, the path of the battue as you Move and Mount. Shoot as soon as the gun has been properly mounted. Do not be tempted to delay because this will give the clay a chance to get under the barrels, thus forcing you to chase it in a very deliberate manner with no guarantee of success.

Do not worry unduly if you do not get a chance to see the clay until it has rolled over and is slicing full tilt to the ground. Needless to say, this is a much more difficult shot to execute properly but your natural ability to bring the gun up to the right point will be more than a match for it. What you must do is pay close attention to the position of your feet and that of the waiting gun barrel. Address yourself to a point just above the place where the plummeting clay will hit the ground and then look up and back to the point you are going to see the arcing target. Fight any and every temptation to let the gun muzzles follow your gaze; by the time you see the clay and respond to it those barrels will be a long way behind and unable to catch and overhaul it before ground level is reached. Instead, hold the barrels well under the place where the clay will appear and, as soon as it arrives, Move laterally and Mount into its path. Squeeze the trigger the moment the stock comes into the shoulder and do not worry about seeing lead. The gun will come to the right position every time. Any hesitancy or uncertainty, though, on the shooter's part will lead to a half-hearted swing and a lost bird so tell yourself that you are going to push the gun into the target and fire in one movement. Be positive and you will break it consistently.

There are times, too, when battues will be encountered which do not roll over until they

Edge-on battues can be broken provided the shooter looks hard at the clay, keeps his head down and tells himself that it will break if he can get the pattern on it.

are well beyond shotgun range and which have to be shot while they are still edge-on to the shooter. It is easy to convince yourself that these fast-moving, flickering targets are virtually impossible to break on account of the tiny surface area that is now exposed to the shot pattern. This might well be credible at long distances where an open pattern can allow it through untouched but any that are at a sensible range will succumb as long as the gun is held straight.

The difficulties that do surface here are normally of the shooter's own making. He does not believe that the clay can be broken and so he does not push himself to hit it; he merely goes through the motions and will doubtless keep his head off the stock to get a better view of what, he knew, was an inevitable outcome. Yet by looking hard at these difficult clays and keeping the head down when the gun has been mounted, a few surprises will accrue. You must also tell yourself that it will break; simply hoping that you will be lucky and chip a piece off is not the way to build up a score. In fact, it is quite amazing how well edge-on battues will break even when caught fair and square in the shot column from an open-bored barrel.

No doubt some scientist has photographed in slow motion how a target breaks up under multiple hits from a swarm of shotgun pellets but it is hard to picture how such a thorough job can be made of a battue flying edge-on through such a holocaust. The most likely explanation is that the first hits unsettle it sufficiently to let other pellets in the string go to work on its underside in an instant with such utterly satisfying results.

A pill-like mini clay alongside 90mm midi and 110mm standard targets.

MINIS

The same set of circumstances must also go to explain why that other special clay target – the mini – meets a similar fate even at respectably long ranges. Close up it looks small enough to get through the holes in even the best-regulated pattern but when covered properly it disappears in a tiny puff of dust – a case of now you see it, now you don't. But of all the so-called specials found on a Sporting range the mini is possibly the least exciting. In physical size it is supposed to represent a snipe but the angles it is thrown at suggest that, really, it is included on the menu as little more than a novelty. Be that as it may, it still has to be broken so the competitive sportsman should treat it with due seriousness and tackle it with the same determination he shows on bigger 'game'.

The trouble with minis is that their tiny size makes them look as though they are travelling faster than they really are and the unwary shooter can run into a number of problems because of that. There is no doubt that in its initial flight this small clay target does cover the ground very smartly but its light weight ensures that it also slows down fairly quickly as well. As a mid-distance target travelling under power, the mini is no more testing than any other clay, but, as the range – and the distance it covers after leaving the trap – increases, so too can the problems. Even when thrown against the sky its small size makes it harder to see properly, and this aspect of visibility can easily add to the illusion that it is also travelling extremely fast. All in all the mini can be a decidedly deceptive proposition.

The temptation is to let its early pace dictate where it should be broken and where the gun must be held. This, and the illusion it creates when it starts to slow down, can all too easily result in the bird being missed handsomely in front, and over the top in the case of a crosser if the background gives no indication as to its real trajectory. With this in mind, it is often no bad thing to watch the clay's latter stages of flight and let these characteristics influence your approach. If, for whatever reason, you should decide to shoot it late on in flight, bear in mind that a slowing clay is one which is also dropping so keep those gun muzzles under its line to prevent shooting over the top. There is certainly no need (if you use a multichoke gun) to screw in a full choke tube to deal with minis within normal Sporting range. A lightly choked barrel will produce sufficiently dense patterns, though you might feel more confident using a cartridge with No. 8 shot to fill in any gaps rather than a trap 7. Close- to mid-range minis will be broken quite comprehensively with skeet 9's.

ROCKETS

These are the heavyweights in the line-up. In overall diameter they are no bigger than 110mm standard clays or battues but where they differ from standard clays is in weight: their thick, heavy construction puts them on a par with rabbits only this time a dished and skirted profile helps to make them fly.

There is little about this type of clay which makes it any harder to hit than any other, but one characteristic which needs to be borne in mind is that its high density means that it can remain under power a little longer than most. Even when it starts to lose speed, the rocket continues to lumber along and loses height more slowly than a normal clay so, if they are presented as a following pair, be careful not to think that the same lead picture will do both justice. It might, but then again, it might not, especially if they are shot late in flight when they are both slowing and dropping. In this case you may find that the lead needed to break the normal will not be sufficient to stop the rocket. But, like the mini, this clay type is rarely seen, and then usually on a FITASC Sporting layout. It is a bit of a beefy customer and is best tackled with a good trap cartridge, especially when presented at distance.

115

90mm MIDIS

For many shooters this slightly smaller clay represents a much more testing challenge than those of standard size and it is easy to see why. Not only is the midi much faster off the trap arm but its weight-to-size ratio means that it has the optimum loading needed to carry it slightly farther than the bigger target and it does so at a fractionally faster overall speed, too. Apparent speed aside, the most dangerous side to its character is its power of mistaken identity: countless sportsmen miss it by a wide margin because they fail to realise that the normal 40-yard clay they are shooting at is, in fact, a 30-yard midi. The moral of this is always to ask before launching into Plan 49b what it is you are actually up against before setting foot on the stand. Do not wait until you have finished

If you are not sure whether the clay is a midi or a standard, ask the referee!

your allocation of five pairs before finding out the horrible truth from a referee who would have gladly put you in the picture had you not rushed past two minutes earlier without asking.

Knowing what you are up against is a great advantage so, if you have got time, walk the course before taking your gun out of the car and look at the targets carefully from as many angles as possible. This does not mean sitting with each trapper either; a great deal can be gleaned by standing away from the shooting position in safe areas and, if a walkway happens to run behind a trap, stand there for a while and watch the target carefully. From the actual shooting stand it might appear to be a rising bird but the view from the back might tell a very different story. Do not dwell too much on what you have seen but store it away for easy reference when it comes to your turn to shoot. If nothing else, you should ascertain what type of target is being thrown on which stand and, even more important, where it is coming from and where it is going. Simple angles and speeds beat more people each shoot than out and out distance, and this is due to nothing else than the fact that they have not taken the slightest notice of the target and their surroundings.

If you do come across a stand where midis are being thrown, do not let their apparent faster speed put you off but, at the same time, think carefully about what you are doing and whether your gun is in the right position. Make sure, too, that you are looking in the right place for the target and that your body weight is nicely forward. Only when you feel ready should you shout 'Pull'. Surprising as it seems, a weak, high-pitched or overly loud call is a sign that the man on the stand is not at all sure about the target coming next.

At this point it might be as well to recap on one or two faults which people trying Maintained Lead for the first time might be exhibiting. The likeliest is gun mount. It is easy when faced with a fast target like a midi to be in too much of a hurry to get the gun mounted and try to maintain the lead deliberately with the stock firmly bedded in the face and shoulder. This is not only undesirable, it is also unnecessary. Compared with other shooting styles, the Move, Mount sequence in Maintained Lead is incredibly slow and works by creating time for the eyes to assess the target and feed the information back to the gun via the shoulders, arms and hands. The presence of a mounted gun in the periphery of a shooter's vision will do nothing but interfere with this all-important eye-to-target relationship.

Equally unproductive is the habit of mounting the gun well ahead of the target only to stop the swing until the clay catches, then passes, the barrels. This sort of indecision both looks clumsy and is clumsy; it is neither one style nor another and should be stopped before it becomes habit forming.

11 Double Trouble

Clay shooting would not be too demanding if Sporting shooters only had to contend with single targets on the shooting range. But, of course, as a discipline English Sporting revolves entirely around the full use of doubles thrown either as simultaneous pairs, following pairs or, more usually, pairs on report. The situation is slightly different in the world of International (FITASC) Sporting where competitors are allowed full use of the gun on targets thrown singly. Even here, though, there is no escape as doubles again enter the arena. So whether we like it or not each of us must come to terms with the fundamental need to master the complexities of combination targets like this before real improvements can be made to our standards of marksmanship. In fact, anybody who is serious in wanting to improve his strike rate must not only be able to cope with doubles, he needs to excel at them.

However, a cursory examination of the yearly Averages Book compiled by the national shooting association reveals the inescapable truth that the average 'average' hovers at around the 55 per cent mark. This is no coincidence. Doubles can have an unsettling influence on people. But throw these same people singles, not pairs, and those paper ratings would take a quantum leap overnight. This tells us something: it is not technique that is lacking in sportsmen who hit, and stick, on a disheartening percentage barrier but an inability to make full and proper use of their skills. Oddly enough, sportsmen hold dear to the view that the reason they do not improve is that they do too little shooting. The feeling is that the more cartridges they push through the barrels the better they will get. To a point this is true but it certainly does not come

anywhere near explaining how thousands of people expending thousands of shells each season still manage to stay firmly stuck on a low average.

To find an answer each of us must look closely at where we go wrong and try to establish whether there is any pattern to why we miss. Do certain angles cause problems? What about the type of combination? How much of the slump is caused by a simple loss of heart when targets are missed? A little bit of self-analysis never hurts; in fact, it has to be the first step on the road to eventual improvement. Unless we identify the places where technique starts to crumble, progress will be severely limited.

Double trouble is such a complex subject that it is difficult to know where to begin but let us start with a very basic shortcoming and say that lack of self-control is at the root of most problems. This can manifest itself in many ways but, when distilled down, the inability to break bigger percentages amounts to little more than misplaced effort and an equal inability to channel technique in the right direction. It certainly is not enough to make a commitment to concentrate harder on the next pair out because the likelihood is that things will only go from bad to worse. By all means concentrate, but just make sure that you are concentrating on the right thing. Before you go on to the stand, stop and ask yourself whether this new-found determination is, in fact, 'concentration' and not merely a smoke-screen behind which hides doubt, uncertainty, even fear. If this is the case, all the mental activity being poured into the problem will likely come to naught and lead, instead, to an inexorable heightening of the deep-seated disappointment and frustration you are trying so hard to beat.

Double trouble can often be traced back to very simple faults. This gentle driven pair has tempted the shooter to pre-mount his gun and come from behind. The fact that his head is off the stock as well is not going to make things any easier.

Determination alone will not lead to success. You must be determined to think about how technique can be used to best effect on the combination you are about to shoot. Oddly enough, the things which hold people back often turn out to be very minor in nature and normally require little work to put right. The hardest part of all is putting a finger on the problem in the first place. Other shooters can help, but beware the advice of sportsmen who are no farther advanced than you. Well-meant comments that you are 'behind that one' or shooting 'over the top' of another are all very well but do nothing to explain why the shot is going where it is. This is where a good coach will really help. What you want to hear from him is 'You missed this because . . .'. Any coach who cannot identify the cause of why you are missing should most definitely be crossed off the list for a return visit. However, even if a suitable tutor is not readily at hand a great deal can be achieved through self-help.

If this is the only option available, then use what you already know about your own technique and start building from there. The first (and most important step) is to recognise that doubles comprise nothing more than two singles. This might sound an over-simplification of the job in hand but, until a sportsman programmes himself to deal with one target at a time and discipline himself accordingly, he can expect to make little or no improvement. In this respect self-control is paramount. Sure signs that it is sadly lacking are easily found and a trip around any Sporting ground will uncover plenty of cases if you want to look for them.

Probably the most common example is where the first bird of a pair is obviously more straightforward than the second, yet the shooter who misses it will unthinkingly move on for the other when a steady second barrel was all that was needed to put the first in the 'bag'. If this second shot also misses the mark, the fault can reasonably be attributed to a suspect technique.

In this situation one of the likeliest causes for such a double miss will be poor foot position, an all too common fault brought about because the shooter has not yet disciplined himself to treat each as a single target and set his feet accordingly. Instead, he is probably trying to adopt a middle-of-the-road stance which, while not exactly favouring the first, will not stop him getting the gun somewhere near the other when the time comes. But compromising the stance in this way is a guaranteed route to below par scores.

Flattering improvements will certainly follow once a shooter makes up his mind to approach each shot singly and let the targets dictate foot position. What, though, of the competitor whose first barrel kills are well up to scratch but whose second shots are in the habit of letting him down, especially in the case of pairs on report?

The two likeliest causes for a double miss here are poor acquisition of the second target brought about, in the main, by uncertainty over where the bird is coming from and where it is going. To be consistently accurate at doubles a shooter needs to know exactly where he should look after shooting the first bird so that he not only sees it at the first time of asking but also brings his gun muzzles

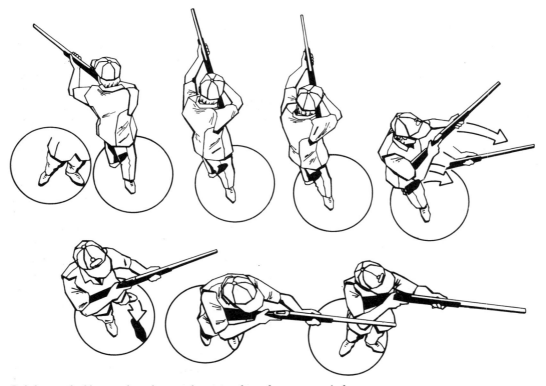

It helps on doubles to adopt the second position for a few moments before turning and addressing the first bird. 'Fixing the image' in this way helps to ensure that once the first shot has been taken you can turn back to the proper position for that second target. Do not try to turn with the gun in the shoulder. Not only will this hamper your chances of seeing the target at the first time of asking, it can also prove highly dangerous should you stumble.

to the right hold point. Nothing should be left to chance here because the shooter who fails to identify his best pick-up point will be left stranded; he will waste valuable moments searching for a target which he knows is 'somewhere in the area' and, worse, his gun will rarely come to rest where it ought to. In fact, there is a strong possibility that between one shot finishing and the next one starting the gun muzzles and the shooter's gaze will separate and end up addressing different places, creating a ragged swing and gun mount as the eye, target and gun struggle to synchronise and get to grips with each other.

Instead, start getting into the habit of thinking about combination targets before you call for them by going through a simple, image-fixing routine on the shooting stand. Visualise the flight of the first target and establish the three ingredients you are already used to with singles: foot position, gun hold and eye contact. Work yourself into position and hold the picture a moment or two before turning to the second target's expected path and go through the same routine again. Make absolutely certain that you have a clear picture of where those feet, gun muzzles and eyes need to be when you turn for the second shot. Hold the image for a few seconds. Now relax, turn back and take up position for the first target, load the gun, call for the bird and kill it. Dismount the gun. Strange as it may seem, your gun and feet will come straight back to that second position automatically, leaving you free to pick up the flight of the bird and to start the Move, Mount, Shoot sequence.

You may find with simultaneous pairs travelling close together that it is not necessary to take the gun out of the shoulder to get speedy and uninterrupted alignment for the second shot, but for any bird which demands a change in foot position it should be done as a matter of course. For one thing, there is always a possibility that on uneven ground you might stumble, and, for another, the mounted gun barrel can interfere with quick,

positive eye/target acquisition. But there is a third, more important, reason for taking the gun out of the shoulder between shots: during the turn the muzzles of a mounted gun do not always follow the shooter's gaze and could end up out of position. In addition to this, the head, through necessity, will have been lifted off the comb as the shooter looks for the bird and there is a danger it will stay off for the second shot. Another drawback, too, is that the man behind the gun might also develop a tendency to direct the gun through arm, rather than, body, movement. While this might not matter too much on targets travelling close together, it should never be tolerated on birds which require a shift in foot position, however slight.

Again, think of each double combination as comprising two single shots and remember how imperative it has been throughout this book to create – and maintain – gun movement by using the power which stems from the hips, waist, chest and shoulders. To recap: if the trunk of the body turns and pivots as a single unit, the head, eyes, arms and gun will have to turn as one too. In other words, where the body and head go, the gun follows, and the easiest way to make sure that it does is to get into the habit of always addressing the body to the target by using the feet as the turning instrument – never the arms and head. What we must guarantee is that when the gun is remounted it is still in direct alignment with the master eye and that the butt of the stock not only slides comfortably home into an open shoulder pouch but the comb also assumes the correct position on the face. This happy state of affairs will not come about if the shooter tries to point the gun with his arms. If, for instance, he lays the gun across his chest to get on to the second bird the shoulder pouch will close down and the butt will end up on the arm socket or bicep; this, in turn, will mean that the head cannot easily assume the right position on the comb of the stock, and eye, barrel, target alignment will suffer as a consequence.

Remember: *always bring the gun to bear on the bird by pivoting the body and turning the feet.*

Valuable lessons can be learnt by watching other people in action and recognising some of your faults in the way they miss targets.

Watching other people in action can be an instructive pastime and throw up a few pointers on how doubles should not be shot. If you see something of yourself in the way others tackle the targets, the lesson will not be wasted, especially if you back up your observations with some careful dry mounting in the privacy of your own home later. Stand in the middle of a room and use the line formed by the walls and ceiling as the flight lines for some imaginary doubles. In this way you can 'shoot' all sorts of angles: crossers, incoming driven, quartering going-away and teal by positioning yourself to take one before turning the feet and body on to the second. You can even work in a few rabbits as well by moving chairs and tables to give a clear line between wall and floor! The value

of dry practice is that the permanent line of the make-believe target will leave you in no doubt as to whether your feet have been placed properly or not. If they have, the gun will stay on line; if not, the muzzles will drift high or low when the gun is mounted and swung. It will also slow or stop if you turn too far back into the second 'shot' by trying to pick up the 'target' as early as possible.

On the shooting ground there is always a temptation to try to shoot the second bird in a double as quickly as possible but this, invariably, is counter-productive; much better to let the bird get a yard or two further out and put in a steady shot than to rush and make a ragged hash of it. Do not fall into the trap either of turning too far back for the second target. While each shot should be

British team member John Woolley has moved into position for a left to right crossing bird on report (in this case an upside-down battue) after taking a driven target in front. The temptation is to bring the gun barrels too far back towards the trap but John has resisted this, rested the muzzles comfortably out in front and, instead, looks left to the point where he knows the bird will appear.

visualised as a single, it should be remembered that between the first bird being killed and the body being turned, that second target will already have been released. It will almost certainly have passed the point where you would have started to Move and Mount had it been the first in the combination, so take this into account when you mentally rehearse the second foot and gun position. In some situations it is quite possible that during the turn the gun will actually pass the target going in the opposite direction, forcing you to stop abruptly, change momentum and race after the bird. The unsettling thing here is not that the barrels have ended up behind the target but that the sudden change in direction unsettles the gun mount, causing the shooter to rush his shot and commit a number of fundamental errors in the process.

In this respect successful doubles shooting has everything to do with getting the visual pick-up point sorted out in your own mind from the outset and engineering a secondary foot position and gun hold that allow you to see the target clearly. It has nothing to do with the head and neck going in search of it on their own so, if you can master the art of directing the gun barrels by body movement, you will be well on the way to breaking many more targets as a consequence.

Highly satisfactory improvements will also be made if the shooter, when faced with simultaneous pairs, disciplines himself to shoot the right target first. But which one is the right target? There is no hard and fast answer to this, only that you should choose the one which favours your own technique and shooting style. For instance, a Follow-Through shooter tackling a pair of targets, say, crossing together from left to right, would come up on the rear one of the two and then swing along to the leader by keeping the momentum of his gun going. The Maintained Lead shooter, on the other hand, will strive to take the front clay first so that the barrels remain ahead of the second one. Of course, there will always be a small percentage of angled targets which put the Follow-Through

shooter in front of the second bird and others that leave the gun barrels behind for a devotee of Maintained Lead. You can minimise the chances of this happening by deciding very carefully which bird you are going to shoot and where you are going to shoot it. But if this does not work out as planned, both will have to recognise the changed circumstances and react accordingly.

If there is a secret in shooting pairs released simultaneously it is in making space for yourself and deciding how best your usual technique can be used to greatest effect. However, from the point of view of Maintained Lead it is as well to bear in mind that, should the targets be tracking along at different heights, it is best to take the lower of the two first and then bring the gun up for the other. It is always easier to mount up to a target than it is to drop the gun down; you reduce the chances of the lower bird being hidden from view by the mounted gun barrel and, also, a rising gun muzzle is much more controllable and will come to the point of aim at the first time of asking.

The situation is slightly different in the case of a pair of springing teal where it is usually best to shoot the higher bird first and then take the other as it comes up the elevated second gun hold. Do not forget, though, to reposition those feet slightly if the trajectory of the second bird is different from the first. It only takes a second to adjust the stance and is far more likely to prove effective than it would by trying to maintain movement using hands and arms on their own.

Much of what I have already discussed in this chapter applies to the successful shooting of pairs released on report of the gun and the same goes for that 'halfway house' combination – the following pair where the trapper reloads, and releases, his machine as soon after the first as he can manage. Both clays follow the same path but it is likely that the course organiser will inject a bit of variety into the proceedings here by throwing, say, a normal target followed by a midi. If this is the case, the shooter needs to be on his guard. What he must do is establish where the second bird is likely to be when he has broken the first. If it is already in view, he must not take the gun back too far to meet it.

The essential element here is one of timing the shot and being able to bring the gun to the secondary hold point at the same time as the eyes go back and pick up the next target. It might be that there is a useful delay in the trapper reloading and getting the second clay airborne, but, again, control the urge to take the gun too far back if the next one out is travelling at a faster speed. The actual difference in hold position between the first and second birds might only be a matter of a few feet but the extra time it gives in responding to the target will be well worth having and might hold the key to success, or failure.

Earlier we mentioned the role that a good coach can play in identifying problems and suggested that if he was not capable of explaining why you miss, he was not worth a return visit. Equally it should be noted that your attitude to instruction will also have a bearing on the outcome of a lesson. Do not go with the intention of showing him how good you are at some targets; show him, instead, how useless you are at the others. Now, you might find that a very obvious conclusion, but the fact has to be faced that some people hate to admit that they need help. It is almost as if they view themselves as personally inadequate in some way or other. If you have a tendency to be like this swallow your pride and be honest from the outset; don't tell a half-truth by hiding the depth of your despair. Bare your soul and go along prepared to listen and act on what you hear and see.

If you are prepared to listen and act on what he has to say, you will be well on the way to overcoming your difficulties. But do not expect overnight miracles. You will probably rush off to a convenient shoot the weekend after the lesson to practise only to find that your modified and polished technique is not dusting the targets in the same way as it did during the lesson. I expect you will feel cheated, but you cannot expect a new move or two to oust old habits straight away – they have to be practised over and over again until they replace the earlier regime. This is especially true if the 'cure' is markedly different to your old style. If it is purely a case of developing and expanding on what you do already, the lesson will sink in quite quickly and easily.

What you should not do is ditch the teaching because it does not work instantly. Give it time and do not be in too much of a hurry to revert back to what you know best – missing. You might well find it useful to book another lesson or two so that the improved technique stays fresh next time you are out on the range.

12 Gun Fit. Does Yours?

Most people never feel the need to have a gun fitted to them. The standard stock on their usual gun is as near a fit as they could dare wish. You might not be as fortunate.

Gunmakers, like clothes designers, have their own ideas about what the average man measures up to and design their wares accordingly. They cannot afford to do it any other way. If they were to make a whole range of different stocks to accommodate every conceivable human shape, production costs would go through the roof and the price of their product would quickly become uncompetitive.

Thankfully, stocks can be bent, twisted, lengthened or shortened quite easily by a skilled gunsmith if a customer finds that his frame is markedly different to what the maker had in mind when he designed his off-the-peg gun. Thankfully, too, it is not very often that major and costly modifications have to be carried out to put things right. Minor, inexpensive, alterations are usually all that is required.

The trouble with gun fitting is that some people see it as a cure-all for missing when often it is their basic technique that is to blame. Before anybody rushes off to the most convenient stock doctor demanding that wood be hacked off here, there and everywhere to straighten things out they should first make sure it really is the gun, not them, that is at fault.

If the trouble is one of style, all that will be achieved by altering the stock is to encourage and accommodate the ailment. In fact, there is little point contemplating stock alterations of any sort until a shooter is absolutely sure he has mastered his gun mounting. This is because fitting only pays if the stock can be brought to the same place in the shoulder and face each time. The same goes for stance. If a shooter lowers or raises his head from one shot to another or alters the way he stands, accurate fitting becomes a difficult proposition. In really bad cases it can prove a near impossibility.

There is a great deal of mystique attached to the whole question of what is a properly fitted gun so it is maybe worth reflecting on the inescapable fact that for every one sportsman who worries and frets about whether his gun is a right fit there are thousands of others shooting happily (and perfectly well) with guns straight off the gundealer's shelf. They might not be a perfect fit but most people, with a little experience, find that they can easily adapt themselves to the imperfections without suffering a loss of form. In this respect the gunmaker's idea of 'Mr Average' is not so inaccurate after all.

This does not mean that you should totally disregard gun fit. It helps to have a basic grasp of what is involved because you are then better able to understand why imperceptible changes to the way you hold the gun or stand for the shot actually work.

Before taking a closer look at the configuration of a stock and how the stance of a sportsman can affect its fit we need to realise that it is shaped the way it is to take account of the human frame. The more we grow away from the gunmaker's idea of Mr Average the more likely it is that we feel the need to do something about the gun. Minor differences can usually be taken in our stride but help certainly should be found if the gun feels uncomfortably awkward to handle. You can be sure that marksmanship is suffering if it does. The main measurements to consider are length, drop and cast.

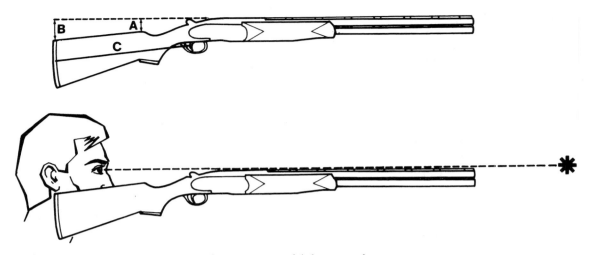

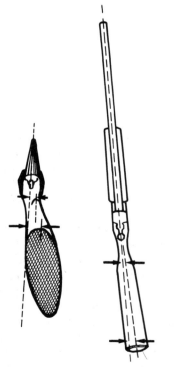

The main measurements to consider on a Sporting gun are (a) drop at comb (b) drop at heel and (c) length of stock. These determine the position of the shooter's eye, both in relation to the rib and to the stock.

Most gun stocks also carry a degree of cast to accommodate the shape of the human face. This allows the eye to assume a position which is central to the barrel rib when the gun is mounted.

VERTICAL MEASUREMENT

The length of a stock determines how easily the gun can be brought into the shoulder pocket. If it is too long the butt plate will show a tendency (exaggerated with bulky clothing) to catch on the shooting coat as the gun is being mounted and lead to the shooter developing an unfortunate habit of 'ducking' his head to the stock. As we have already seen, the correct way is to bring the wood to the face first and bed everything together by gently 'pushing' the shoulder into the butt plate a fraction later.

The combination of an over-long stock and head dipping will often give rise to a number of unavoidable errors. Each, on its own, is sufficient to cause a run of misses. Put them all together and we have a recipe for long-term frustration.

Good shooting relies on a fluid swing with the mounted gun. If a shooter is forced to 'crunch' his head down to meet the stock, the muscles in his neck and shoulders will tighten and restrict movement of the gun to an appreciable degree. A gun butt that comes to rest below the shoulder pouch and leaves the

This gun is too low in the comb and too long in the stock. The butt is coming to rest too low in the shoulder pouch forcing the shooter to hunch down on the wood. Not only will the swing be affected but the ball of the right thumb will bang back into his nose and face under recoil.

shooter no option but to take his head to the comb of the stock is one which will tend to shoot above the point of aim.

This disadvantage is further compounded by the tendency for an over-long stock to end up sitting on the upper arm, not in the shoulder pocket. This trait is more usual in people with broader than average chests. They find it difficult to slide the gun into their shoulder so, instead, they simply lift it clear of their armpit, straight on to the arm and shoulder socket. Not only can this lead to bruising but it also tends to put the angle of the barrel slightly across the shooter's line of vision, causing a right-hander to shoot to the left of the target.

The problems might not necessarily end there. With the gun stock clear of the shoulder pouch there is a likelihood that under recoil and without the body backing up to absorb its rearward travel the butt will slip further

down the arm, causing any second barrel shot to go hopelessly awry. And on top of this, there is a fair possibility that the long-stock sufferer will also have to cant his head over the stock to get his eye into position.

Not only does this severely handicap his chances of delivering an accurate shot but the likelihood increases of the stock banging into his jaw and cheek when the cartridge goes off. Canting the head in this fashion also means that the shooter's cheek will not make proper contact with the stock, thus making first-time alignment with the barrel and eye a very uncertain proposition.

It is not unusual to find people struggling with guns carrying too much length trying to lessen the problems by bringing their left hand ever farther back on the fore-end. This, within reason, will help by allowing the left arm to push the gun butt clear of the armpit and so reduce the risk of the gun snagging

The fit of this gun does not suit the user's stance; to get the comb into his face he has had to cant his head – a fault which has put his master eye out of alignment with the rib. The gun will have a tendency to shoot right of the mark.

the clothes or dragging on the chest. But there is a point at which the ploy ceases to be a help and, instead, becomes a hindrance; that point is reached when the cheek of the shooter ends up so far back on the stock that when the gun is mounted the master eye drops below the line of the barrel rib.

Equally, a stock that is too short should also be avoided. Whereas the man who uses an excessively long stock will have a tendency to favour a short left-hand reach, the other will lengthen his grip to get around its shortcomings. This ploy will work, provided the lack of length does not leave his face resting against, or just behind, the right hand holding the mounted gun; during recoil the ball of the thumb can move smartly back and deliver a sharp, painful reminder to the shooter's nose that all is not well with this particular stock.

Users of short-stocked guns may also be tempted to compensate for the lack of length

by assuming a squarer stance to the target. This too can help to a point but it needs to be remembered that the more a shooter turns towards the target the greater becomes the need to have the stock cast to retain that all-important eye-barrel alignment on which all shooting styles rely. The unavoidable consequence of using a gun with insufficient cast and an open stance is to leave the eye looking down the left-hand side of the gun instead of down the centre of the rib. In an attempt to create the right sight picture, a shooter must again cant his head to get his cheek on the top of the stock – and in the process create unwanted tension to his neck and shoulders.

In this situation head canting is well nigh unavoidable. If the eye remains to the left of the barrel, the shot, when it is let loose, will miss the target to the left.

One last, and often painful, consequence of shooting with a gun with far too short a stock comes in the actual gun mount itself.

(Right) With the gun mounted comfortably into the face and shoulder the eye should assume a position directly over the rib of the gun.

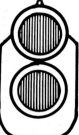

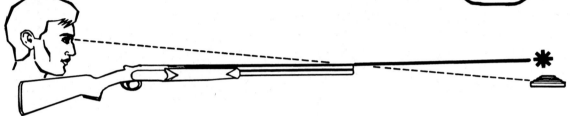

(Above) If the eye assumes a position too high on the rib, the muzzles will have a tendency to shoot high as well . . .

(Right) . . . similarly, if a shooter rolls his head over the stock, putting his master eye to the right of the rib, the gun will have a tendency to shoot to the right as well.

131

If you feel that your own gun is too high in the comb insert pieces of paper between the barrel and standing breech. Keep adding slivers until the rib is in direct alignment with your eye. A gunsmith can lower the wood if you feel that it will help your shooting.

Instead of lifting the stock to the face and shoulder in one motion a sportsman will show a tendency to pull the gun back to his shoulder when the stock touches his cheek. Quite apart from upsetting the gun mounting rhythm, this secondary action can also prove a painful operation by allowing the gun to recoil back with unchecked momentum.

Earlier we drew the analogy that a shot-gunner's master eye fulfilled the same function as the backsight on a rifle, i.e. its position relative to the muzzle of the gun determines how high it will shoot to the point of aim. The diagrams here show how the gun muzzle will respond if the dominant eye assumes an ever higher position over the barrel. It pulls the muzzle upward and so raises the gun's point of impact.

The determining factor here is the drop that a gunmaker chooses to give to the comb and heel of his stock; in his mind Mr Average might have the centre of his eye set 1¾ inches above the underside of his cheek, so he fashions the comb of his gun in a way that he thinks will place the model's eye directly over the rib of the gun when the stock is mounted, assuming, of course, that the stock is the right length in the first place.

If the gun is to shoot to the same place consistently, a shooter's face must assume the same position on the stock every time the gun is mounted. What is the 'right' position?

Before starting to mount the gun it is desirable to assume a stance which will encourage the head to 'push' forward slightly when the stock meets the shooter's face. The surest – and neatest – way of doing this is to shift your balance in favour of the front foot.

Not only will it encourage the head to bed itself comfortably on to the stock, but the forward weight will help ensure that it stays in position and not be inclined to lift and pull the muzzles with it. The cheek wants to take up position just behind the right hand, but not so close as to run the risk of being bumped by the ball of the thumb when the gun recoils back into the shoulder. It should not be so far back as to make the shooter adopt an overly upright head position; a point nudging slightly forward of the comb's mid-position is normally the most comfortable and secure place for most people.

The difference in comb height on standard Sporting guns is unlikely to vary more than ⅛ or ¼ inch between makers but it is surprising what difference these can make to the gun's point of aim. A ¼-inch elevation at the breech end might not seem very much on paper but 35 yards up-range the distance between the target and the centre of the shot pattern may be 15 inches or more.

A shotgun's point of aim is usually determined by measuring the gap between the centre of the shot pattern and an aiming mark painted against a large steel plate 40 yards from the shooter. The gun is mounted at the mark, shouldered and fired without hurry but without conscious delay to check the alignment of the rib with the eye. A gun that 'shoots to the point of aim' is generally accepted as being one which centres its pattern about nine inches over the mark; such a gun will help its user cover a rising target without handicapping him should the clay be coming down, not up. It is no coincidence that a gun displaying these characteristics will place the stock comfortably in the cheek and position the master eye directly over the top of the rib.

Some clay shooters who come from behind the target prefer using guns that shoot higher than this so that on everything but driven targets (where the clay is blotted out anyway) they can keep the target in view over the barrel and judge their lead accordingly. Such guns will have slightly higher combs than most and hence place more of the shooter's eye above the rib.

All the guns here (apart from the trap model second right) are standard production Sporting models. Note the differences in comb height.

This no doubt works well for them but it is not a formula that should tempt anybody using Maintained Lead. This is because the hands bring the muzzles of the gun into the plane in which the eyes are looking, and a gun that throws its charge too high will prove a severe handicap.

It becomes a particularly unforgiving beast for people who have to cheek the gun firmly and deliberately on the first shot to ensure that their eye is directly on the rib so that they are shooting to where they are looking. They succeed in powdering the clay with the first shot, dismounting their gun to get on to the second of a pair but, in the hurry to catch it before it gets too far away, let loose as soon as the woodwork brushes the cheek. Because they have not cheeked it as hard as they did

for the first shot, their eye assumes a higher position over the rib causing the gun to shoot over the top of the bird.

This will happen regardless of target speed and angle; however, it is more likely to occur with high birds (tower crossers particularly) as the shooter's natural reaction is to lift his head slightly during the mount to look at the bird.

HORIZONTAL MEASUREMENT

Very few gun stocks when viewed from above run in a direct straight line with the centre of the rib. Most, if not all guns for Sporting, will display a certain amount of lateral displace-

A gun-fitter takes the measurements off an adjustable try gun and applies them to his client's own weapon.

ment called 'cast' – a measurement given by the stock maker to try to accommodate the face of the shooter and the position of his shoulder pocket. Both physical features have a tendency to take the centre of the butt away from the 'aiming' eye. Cast helps to ensure that it continues to align with the centre of the rib when the gun has been mounted. Again, the amount of cast given to a gun is measured in fractions of an inch; only when a shooter shows signs of greater left eye domination or when both are equally strong (a condition known as central vision) will a stock have to carry appreciable cast to maintain eye/rib alignment.

Most experienced shooters can tell within moments of picking up a new or strange gun whether it fits them or not. They know instinctively whether it mounts easily and to where they are looking and, if it does not, they can (and will) make minute adjustments accordingly.

Only if the gun shows a tendency to try to override their instincts might they feel it necessary to have work done which will cancel out the disadvantage. They probably know what needs to be done to the gun to correct its faults but they might decide to seek the second opinion of an expert gun-fitter with a try gun just to confirm their suspicions.

The try gun is a normal gun with a stock that can be quickly lengthened, shortened, raised, lowered and cast with the help of a screwdriver and spanner. In the hands of a fitter who knows what he is doing such a gun can be used to get a fairly accurate set of measurements which his customer can then have transferred to his own gun.

Even the most expert gun-fitter in the world, though, can only recommend a fit based on his client's style of shooting on the day (or days) the fitting process takes place. If, at a later stage, he drifts into using a more open (or closed) stance to the one his fitter took into account, the fit will be affected accordingly.

Changing stance will change the position of the eye in relation to cast more than any other single feature of gun fit, though the more the shooter drifts from his original style the more likely it is that other considerations will come into play.

If stance can affect the position of the eye in relation to the barrel, it must also be remembered that the position of the left hand will affect the fit of the gun in terms of stock length. In other words, you should always grip the fore-end of the gun in the same place to ensure its predictably smooth arrival into the shoulder pocket.

Pay equal attention too to your right hand. While the left is mainly instrumental in guiding the gun on to the target and pushing the stock clear of the armpit, the right carries out the important job of lifting the stock into position and controlling the gun once it is in the shoulder and being fired.

Fitting a stock can be a complicated process; so complicated, in fact, that you should not be too surprised if you go to a number of professional fitters or shooting coaches and find that each reach a very different conclusion about what your needs are.

Strange as it may seem, some instructors – and some fitters for that matter – pay too little attention to the way a poorly shaped grip can affect the fit of an individual's gun or, more importantly, the ease and consistency with which he can mount it. Much can depend upon the size of the shooter's hands and especially the length of his fingers.

Watch a good shot in action and you will notice that his elbows stay below the level of the gun, especially the elbow of the right arm. From this position the gun stock can be lifted effortlessly up and into the shoulder and remain securely in place both during and after the cartridge has been fired. A 'dropped' elbow also allows an easy swing.

The easiest way of ensuring that the elbow does not interfere with the way the gun is mounted is to hold the stock towards the back of the grip and stretch the index finger up to the trigger. The blade of this should rest in the finger's first joint.

Again, gunmakers have done a fairly good

135

Shooting clothes can affect the fit of a gun in no small way. This shooter is well wrapped up to keep out the winter chill with a bulky sweater but, if the gun was fitted in the height of summer, the extra padding will tend to lengthen the stock. Minor changes to the position of the left hand might be needed to counteract the changed circumstances.

job of shaping the pistol-grip stock on their competition guns to suit most people, but anybody with longer, or shorter, digits than 'average' should pay some attention to detail. This is particularly important for anybody with short fingers because, in an effort to take up the correct trigger position, there is often a tendency to push the hand higher up the grip toward the top lever and trigger guard. This can automatically raise the elbow and so hinder the mount, and lead to the butt taking up an inconsistent position in the shoulder. In fact, the by-product of such a grip can be quite similar at times to that of an over-long stock so, again, the shooter should satisfy himself that it is not the hand position which is at fault before asking for wood to be removed.

Some manufacturers recognise that the length of people's fingers do vary and have fitted their guns with easily adjustable triggers. With the help of a small turn-screw or Allen key, the owner of such a gun can slide the trigger back and forth to suit. What is not so easily overcome is the size of a shooter's palm in relation to the width and depth of the grip itself. Again, the man with short hands will be more disadvantaged if the actual woodwork fills his hand too well. Such a stock coupled with a deep grip really can cause problems. Again, however, they are not insurmountable. A practical gunsmith can take wood out of the grip without weakening the stock.

It has become fashionable in recent years to produce Sporting guns with a device called a palm swell. This ensures that the hand assumes the same position on the grip shot after shot and improves stability during recoil.

Palm swells might be very useful on trap guns where the gun is shouldered carefully before the bird is called for but they are an unnecessary feature in Sporting where mobility and freedom of movement is paramount to good shooting. All is well if the palm swell suits the shape of the shooter's hand but if it does not it can throw the hand into the wrong position and, in all probability, raise the elbow in the process.

Similarly, guns that are too thin in the grip should also be treated with a degree of caution because under recoil the hand might slide forward. This is not too bad on single shots but, if the gun is dismounted before the shooter moves on to a second target, the mount, as we have seen, might be affected.

Very few clay shooters use double-trigger guns nowadays. These are guns which required the user to move his hand slightly to get his finger from one trigger to another without interruption. Straight hand stocks allowed him to do this. However, the fashion now is for a single trigger firing both barrels in a sequence chosen by the shooter so the prerequisite is for a form of pistol grip which holds the hand steady. My feeling is that too many gunmakers have gone a little too far in this respect and stocked their Sporting models with grips which are too full and deep.

This has made otherwise excellent guns too much of a handful in a sport where ready eye-to-hand co-ordination is highly desirable. Again, personal preference plays a part in the gun an individual will choose and while I now shoot a gun with a slim pistol grip, I often have a hankering to go back to my first Browning with its single trigger and straight hand stock. The answer, probably, is a compromise in the shape of gently rounded semi-pistol grip which aids pointability by keeping the hand as close to the centre of the gun as possible and allowing the shooter some leeway in choosing the hand position that suits his gun-mounting style.

Similarly, slimness is also a desirable feature in the fore-end wood in that the closer we can get to the gun's centre of axis the better we can direct it on to the target.

From all this it might appear that gun fit is a complicated subject, but this really is not so. As long as you feel comfortable with an off-the-peg gun there is little point trying to find excuses for missing by blaming the gun at every opportunity. Only if it feels awkward to handle or mount and forces you to make allowances in the way you stand should expert advice be sought.

13 Practice Makes Perfect

Who needs practice? As a shooting-ground proprietor I suppose I have a vested interest in seeing all my stands working to capacity on practice nights. As such it is very tempting to say that practice sessions are the best things that were ever devised! And so they are, provided a shooter has a clear picture of what he is trying to achieve by doing a tour of the shooting field and working his way through a couple of boxes of cartridges in the process.

If all he is looking for is a great deal of fun and relaxation, he should be positively encouraged to make full use of any facilities available to him in his area. But once a shooter decides he needs practice because he

Club practice nights are social, friendly occasions. They are also ideal opportunities for careful training sessions as long as the shooter goes along with a clear idea of what he is trying to achieve.

is continually running into problems with certain types of target, or finds that his gun mount and swing are letting him down, the subject can take on a much more serious aspect.

This is because if practice is to achieve anything it must be constructive. There is absolutely no point in turning up at a shooting ground, heading for a problem stand and merrily blowing away fifty shells without thought. Of course, you will feel better for having exercised your shoulders and trigger finger a little – but have you learnt anything? Practice is meaningless unless a shooter is absolutely clear in his mind what he wants to achieve. In Chapter 11 we discussed the need to be positive in the way we approach our sport and this same rule applies with practice birds. Nothing has changed. If anything, the resolve to straighten things out should be very much harder.

Yet it is so easy to get side-tracked on a practice session. For example, you might be setting off from the clubhouse towards the trap throwing incoming quarterers (or whatever) when suddenly two or three friends pull alongside and suggest that you should all go around together. You do not want to risk offending them so you agree. Where is that sense of resolve and positive application now?

Let us suppose, though, that you do make it to the stand alone and have the trapper all to yourself without other people pressing you to hurry up, finish your allocation and let them have a go. Have you established what you are trying to do or are you simply going to bang away until you are out of cartridges and it is time to go home? Whatever you might think, this is a very valid point to raise because some people do honestly believe that if they go through the motions often enough they will eventually realise what they are doing wrong and will cure themselves. This rarely, if ever, happens. In fact, the opposite is more likely to be true: practising for its own sake normally only ever results in a shooter staying right where he is. His

'problem' could even worsen, particularly if his negative approach results in even more of these bogey birds being missed.

Evidence that this is true is all around us. You need only look at how regular practice sessions have helped some of your friends. Which of them has gone up a class or two in the last year or so? How many are still no farther forward than they were this time last season? If any have progressed, they deserve closer attention and it would be well worth tagging along to let some of their positive thinking rub off on your own shooting. Talk to them, watch them shoot, take note of what they do and ask yourself whether there is anything in their approach that can help improve your own scores.

From this you might think that I am straying a little from the path of practice, but I am not. I am trying to stress the point that meaningful gains in performance can be made only by working on our own technique. Coaches, magazine articles and books can help provide some of the answers and the impetus here but that is all they can do. They are merely outside influences which can point a shooter in the right direction and provide some support as he negotiates the problems that will surely lie before him.

In the end it is a shooter's own technique and the way he applies that knowledge which breaks targets. Nothing else. Any problems that do crop up and demand of the shooter that practice is needed are signs that some part of the technique is letting him down. And if we are agreed that technique is the key to success then where is the point in practice if it is not being focused on this all-powerful part of the story? If the technique is wrong then there is precious little hope of doing anything other than practising the fault when you take yourself off to some quiet corner to put matters right.

If you do decide to supplement your usual weekly quota of targets by ironing out faults with an additional helping of pitch and chalk, make your mind up to be as methodical as possible. Do not try to do too much at once.

Single out the problem birds and concentrate on one at a time. Little will be gained by popping off a dozen or so shells at one stand and then scurrying round two or three more, repeating the exercise before the ground closes for the day. On the other hand, do not overdo it by cementing yourself to the stand and firing away until your arms ache. Physical tiredness will simply reflect in your mental well-being. If eyes and brain are jaded, the reflex signals which direct the gun will, by implication, be affected too. Instead, turn this quest for practice into something of a training schedule: split things down into easily managed units and take a few minutes' break to go over what you have just done before picking up the gun again.

Remember that you are trying to sharpen up your technique, so tackle the stand in the way that you normally would: decide where you want to break the target and put your feet in a position to do so. Make your mind up about the gun hold position and the point where you see the clay clearly, then call for the bird. Have five shots and take a break.

Let us assume that you chipped two and missed the other three. The first thing to remember is not to let yourself slump into despondency. Take strength from the fact that your basic technique breaks other targets and angles well enough so tell yourself that it will only be a matter of time before this one too starts meeting the same fate. Think about the two you did hit. Can the way they broke tell you anything? No? Then try another five shots by altering your stance slightly; try shooting it a bit later by turning those feet another inch or two further round and adjust the eye position/gun hold accordingly to give yourself more time to see it and react. Still no joy? You feel that you are missing in front? Then shift position again by turning into the target this time, move the gun a little closer to the point where the clay is seen clearly and try again. Now we are getting somewhere – you took the top edge off four of the five. Try holding the gun a little bit lower to its line of flight. The next four are powdered and the fifth clean missed. You have obviously found the answer and that last target would have gone the same way had you not taken it for granted but cheeked the gun stock properly.

At this point you might not wish to push your luck and will no doubt be sorely tempted either to end there or inject a bit of variety into the proceedings by moving to another trap. Don't! Stay put and shoot several more. Only this time try to memorise that fleeting barrel-to-target relationship that comes just as the trigger is squeezed and the clay breaks up into pieces. Do not be tempted to transfer your gaze from the clay to the barrel itself because this will cause you to slow (or stop) the swing of the gun and miss the target. When the shooter is concentrating on the clay the line of the rib appears as nothing more than an indistinct blur on the periphery of his vision. Nonetheless, it is an important blur. Remember it and commit this positive picture to memory. Once it is locked in, it can be drawn on time and time again when circumstances repeat themselves. Recalling this image will become an integral part of technique and, as such, will rarely fail the shooter provided he gives it free rein.

The human brain might well be an incredibly complicated machine able to store limitless instructions and information but it does have one failing: it is unable to cope with more than one or two reflex instructions at a time, so do not overload it by trying to do too much in one session. Concentrate on imprinting the technique and sight picture needed to handle one problem at a time and move on to another only when you are sure that the solution to the first is permanently recorded. Pay attention to the constituent parts of the Move, Mount, Shoot sequence and work on them until you can break them without conscious thought. But be careful not to tire yourself in the process. If you start to feel as though the targets are being broken on 'auto pilot', stop. You have reached a stage where there is precious little concentration being applied and mistakes can creep in, colouring the positive image already created.

If you have got a style which works well on particular types of target then there is little point changing for change's sake.

While this book is mainly concerned with explaining how targets can be broken with Maintained Lead, it should be borne in mind that some people 'mix and match' their style to suit different targets and angles. It is not that they cannot break them with one particular style, but just that they feel more confident tackling it by slipping into another mode when the occasion arises. As we have already seen, clay shooters do have the luxury of knowing where a target is coming from and where it is going and, by setting up a practice stand to suit, they can reproduce any speed and angle they want to. They can thus set about trying different styles and settling on one which they feel most comfortable with. Blind adherence to one style of shooting is both limiting and counter-productive so if progress is not made by following a routine which can usually be relied on with other targets, try something else and compare the results. As a Maintained Lead shooter you might find it more reward-ing to come from behind a problem target, just as a Follow-Through shooter could make similar improvements by starting with the muzzles in front of a target which normally manages to fox him.

No chapter on practice targets would be complete without taking a cursory look at the role a simple hand-operated clay trap can play in improving a shooter's all-round ability; the sort of single-arm trap which can be carried (complete with stand) in the boot of a car and erected within minutes in some quiet corner of a farmer's field – provided permission has been given, of course! With a little bit of imagination even the cheapest machine can be used to throw a variety of targets and liven up the usual staple diet of a fast single or slow, spreading, double that the arm has been designed to throw. I hope one day trap manufacturers will supply each machine with a list of hints and suggestions about what other target combinations can be thrown by exercising a little ingenuity.

141

Portable traps like this Universal can be carried easily in a car boot and erected within minutes. With a little bit of imagination it can be used to recreate all sorts of different speeds and angles.

Wooded hillsides, valleys and clearings are all very well if an individual or small club has access to such features but extra variety can be had quite easily from a single-arm trap placed in the middle of a flat grass field. The trouble is that unless you know one or two 'tricks of the trade' the decision to put on a testing target in these sort of circumstances all too soon comes back to the trap spring being tightened down as far as possible and an incredibly fast clay being launched. Somehow such impromptu set-ups always seem to lack the sparkle that some other clubs and grounds manage to achieve, even though the equipment they use is no different (in some cases worse!) than the trap you possess. When people talk about simple traps they almost invariably conjure up pictures of a machine that can only throw standard clays in the fashion already described. Yet with a little bit of thought – and maybe a home-made spring clip or two – there is no reason why more of us cannot reproduce those loping quartering clays, curling droppers, looping

Even single-arm traps can be used to throw doubles.

142

A simple piece of aluminium sheet, a sprung wire clip and a few self-tapping screws can extend the role of many single-arm traps.

battues and skimming doubles that so tantalise us at some other grounds.

It is certainly worth experimenting with your own trap because it is then possible to recreate the target angles and speeds which cause the most problems and so allow you to improve your technique with meaningful practice. Some years ago we both compiled an article for *Sporting Gun* magazine which explained ways in which sportsmen could add a little extra spice to the proceedings. Very little has changed since then so it is well worth quoting extracts here from the original:

If you take a walk around High Lodge Shooting School you will see that most of the traps in regular use are honest to goodness over-centre arms chosen for reliability and simple maintenance with a preference toward Fareys and Bowmans in single- and double-arm configuration. The double arms are left pretty much to their own devices but the ground has carried out a few minor modifications to the singles – alterations which anybody with access to an electric drill and some self-tapping screws can effect quite easily. What [John] does is to fit a clip made from either sheet aluminium or sprung wire so that some double clay combinations can be launched from single arms. Factory-fitted rubber guide rails on the arm remain in place.

For instance, most single arms can be used to throw a spreading double but by adding a clip in the right place clays can be sat one on top of the other, such as a pair of midis which, instead of spreading, now travel together at the same speed. This ploy is particularly effective as a Springing Teal combination from a lever-operated Farey. All John has done to ensure that each pair of targets is consistent is to reposition one of Farey's own sprung wire clips (cost about £1.50) to hold the clays in place on the near vertical arm. Similar wire clips are also fitted to the bottom rail of some double arms so that a midi can be launched alongside either a standard or battue on the top deck. The trapper can now throw target combinations which are

A sprung wire fitted to the bottom arm of a doubles trap creates even greater versatility.

not only different in terms of angle . . . but also subtly different in speed. It is this last factor that catches people out time and time again.

Some variations don't even need modified clips. One target John's customers love to shoot is a going-away bird launched from a trap adjacent to them and which then curls back toward the safety cage. Depending on the strength of the spring (or position of the trap), this can either settle in front of the shooter or slant over his head as a dropping driven bird. To duplicate it yourself try tilting the trap a few inches to one side and throw the clay on a rising trajectory away from the shooting position. Once the clay nears its summit it will bank round in a wide arc before heading back toward the waiting shooter. You don't need much tilt to throw this target, and a slight channel or hole dug under one leg of the stand is quite sufficient but if you can come up with a secure way of tipping it a degree or two to one side then several other target types can be thrown as well. The obvious of course is a bolting rabbit, but by sorting out the elevation you can also 'lob' midis and standards; as a crossing shot these appear 'full face' to the shooter and describe a testing arc across the sky.

One bird which really can liven up the proceedings at any Sporting shoot is the battue. So much so that you

Two battues fit snugly under the rubber rail of an arm designed to accommodate the rim depth of a standard-size clay.

When throwing battues always choose an arm with a broad blade. This supports the clay during compression. The clay on the left has no support and will break.

wonder why more clubs and grounds don't use them. You will often read in advertisements that 'such and such a trap' is supplied with a special battue arm but the truth is that most standard single arms can also be used quite effectively. This is especially so when it comes to throwing doubles: the combined depth of two battues is about the same as the rim on a standard clay and, as such, will sit comfortably between the blade and the rubber rail. At a pinch you can also throw singles but this is where a light home-made clip comes into its own. Best results come from using a broad-bladed arm which supports the clay as it is being launched. If the blade is too narrow then the wafer thin battue hangs over the edge and will break during the launch.

Battues thrown in the normal way will travel a long distance very quickly, slicing through the air in spectacular fashion. But at High Lodge, John is fond of ringing the changes . . . by loading a battue upside down on the arm. This too travels fast but when it's about a third into its flight it does a victory roll and plummets to the ground. This is a tricky one to shoot because the shooter has got to time his mount and shot to perfection.

We have included a number of photographs here which clearly show a few of the options open to the owner of a so-called simple trap. It helps of course if you have got several that can be pressed into service but there is no reason why one or, better still, two, single-arm traps cannot be used more imaginatively by a group of friends getting together for a bit of practice. The only way to find out is to try a few different things and see what happens. Who knows, you might even discover a few tricks that nobody else has yet thought about!

14 You must be Mental

Success in clay shooting is a very personal thing. Some people set out with dreams of winning a national championship, others hanker after honours at a lower level, while still more tell themselves that they would be happy enough settling for a better score than the one they got the previous week at the club get-together.

Those people with a genuine and deep-seated aversion to competition – and there are plenty – probably cannot understand why anybody should actually want to pit themselves against other sportsmen, let alone revel in the experience in the way that they do. They would rather be gardening, shopping . . . doing anything at all so long as it meant not having to pitch against other people. To them the word competition is anathema.

Yet, regardless of the type of shooting we do and the aspirations we might hold, all of us harbour a competitive streak. It is more highly developed, of course, among people who actively seek 'confrontation' with others as a way of measuring their skills and maybe gaining some recognition along the way, but retiring types too relish a battle. Only with them it is a private affair waged against themselves.

It is called self-improvement. We all want a slice of it. Anybody who says otherwise is being dishonest. Once a clay shooter loses all

Competition means many things to many different people. Most of the people queueing here for an entry at a big shoot have not got a hope of winning a prize, but the day will not have been wasted if they manage to beat their previous best score.

desire to improve he might as well sell his guns, get rid of his cartridges and turn to some other hobby that reawakens his interest. The point here is that shooting is a game of skill and while bettering your previous score or classification is not, in itself, a means to an end, it is a yardstick by which enjoyment can be measured. Try telling the chap who averages 10 ex 25 at Sporting that his enjoyment of the game would not increase one iota if, instead of 10's, he regularly started to hit 22's. There is no prize for guessing what his answer would be.

Similarly, the man who does shoot high scores at Sporting will (if his competitive edge remains intact) enjoy bumping up his average and, in the process, tap new reserves of satisfaction.

There is plenty of satisfaction waiting to be had out there. This can clearly be seen by the fact that in 1988 there were almost 4,000 people in Britain who went to the time, trouble and expense of shooting in competitions which were registered by their national association and which led to a classification based on the average number of 'kills' achieved by each competitor. Of these, only 194 people (yes, 194!) shot well enough to make AA Class status; less than 1,000 were graded in A Class, while the remainder finished up in B and C Class. By far the biggest proportion were classified C. As you see, plenty of room for improved enjoyment!

While the 4,000 total falls far short of the actual number of Sporting shooters in Britain, the percentage breakdown is pretty indicative of the scores that a travelling gun can expect to encounter at any shoot (registered or otherwise) he cares to enter whether it is here or in America, France, Portugal, Germany, Australia, South Africa, Cyprus or Switzerland. If target standards are universally uniform (as they are in trap and skeet shooting), an A Class Sporting shot in Britain would simply find himself in familiar territory were he to emigrate in an attempt to improve his lot and start figuring in competition results.

Non-improvement is a shooter's worst nightmare. You know you are capable of better scores. It is just that you always seem to end up shooting at grounds where the targets are not to your liking, they use too many midis, one of the referees invariably upsets you and breaks the rhythm or the background is off-putting. Then there is the man for whom 'if only' will be his final epitaph. 'If only' they hadn't used battues, the sun had been better, that slow trapper hadn't broken his concentration, he'd brought his other gun . . . the list is endless.

It is a great shame that so many people fill the lower classifications and stay there. Such people might well enjoy a little bit of success on the way but they never really get on top of their problems and make a break into a higher category. What is even more of a shame is the fact that 99.9 per cent of them should not even be there: watch them shoot and it is clear that they have grasped the fundamentals well enough to be breaking a great many more targets than they are doing. Their gun mount and swing is neat and tidy and they know enough about correct foot position to give themselves a better-than-average chance of connecting with the targets. In fact, if marks were given for artistic impression AA Class would be suddenly bursting at the seams and C Class a virtual desert save for the man enjoying his first outings with a gun. So what is holding so many back?

To say that people do not believe in their own abilities is an over-simplification, but the truth of the matter is that far too many sportsmen restrict and slow their improvement because their mental attitude is wrong. Too many let themselves be driven by negative thoughts. They worry about targets before they even reach the shooting ground. They find it difficult to control anxiety. They do not know how to relax. But above all else, they set themselves unrealistic goals.

A better way of describing this is to say that people have a habit of letting their competitive hopes and aspirations run ahead of them. The confirmed negative thinker knows that he has got the technical ability to

22010	B	BARRINGER L	( )	375	62.4
40214	C	BARRINGTON MD	( )	200	53.5
40231	A	BARROW CR	( )	175	73.1
44533	B	BARTHOLOMEW SM	( )	675	68.0
38572	C	BARTON D	( )	200	50.5
48398	C	BARTRAM A	(L)	100	30.0
32247	B	BARTRUM MJ	( )	150	62.6
48362	C	BASFORD SJ	( )	100	47.0
00883	A	BASHAM S	( )	400	75.7
43809	AA	BASS AP	( )	100	81.0
44348	C	BASSETT BRETT A	(J)	300	40.6
49290	A	BASSETT HK	( )	475	70.3
44347	C	BASSETT RF	( )	300	45.3
45543	C	BATE AC	(L)	500	41.4
40081	C	BATE AD	( )	100	46.0
21201	C	BATE C	( )	225	52.8
48090	C	BATEMAN G	( )	100	28.0
27305	B	BATES DM	( )	100	62.0
26518	C	BATH KP	( )	200	44.0
43913	C	BATH PL	( )	200	45.0
48259	C	BATT GA	( )	100	48.0
21797	C	BATTER JE	( )	100	50.0
47779	C	BAUGHAN R	( )	600	51.5
48429	C	BAXTER B	( )	300	55.6
44607	A	BAYLEY JW	( )	300	76.6
30998	B	BAYLEY SL	(L)	1200	66.7
53069	B	BAYLISS S	( )	200	61.0
27306	B	BAYNTON JR	( )	100	67.0
29929	A	BEAGLEY KG	( )	1200	71.7
30504	C	BEAL GD	( )	100	51.0
09532	B	BEALES D	( )	100	65.0
47723	C	BEALES RJ	( )	100	42.0
30677	A	BEAMISH AJ	( )	800	73.5
34307	A	BEAMISH J	( )	800	71.5
22180	AA	BEAN JK	( )	300	81.3
13194	A	BEARD T	( )	750	71.4
13614	A	BEARDMORE CR	( )	1100	77.4
53017	C	BEARDSLEY P	( )	100	49.0
07516	B	BEARE A J	( )	1275	69.5

12719	C	BEENEY MS	( )	100	56.0
16400	A	BEESE CD	( )	100	74.0
47318	A	BEEVER LJ	( )	100	56.0
02116	A	BEKKERS LA	( )	100	71.0
04852	B	BELL F	( )	200	61.0
50916	B	BELL PJ	( )	400	62.2
12776	A	BELL RC	( )	300	63.0
42374	A	BELL TR	( )	1165	77.6
38024	A	BELLAMY T	( )	100	77.0
45073	A	BELLI A	( )	800	70.3
38612	B	BENN R	( )	100	46.0
28465	C	BENNETT CA	(L)	300	44.3
19512	C	BENNETT PN	( )	750	58.0
33499	C	BENNETT RD	( )	100	54.0
05151	A	BENSON A	( )	300	70.0
43339	B	BENSON RM	( )	100	65.0
46532	B	BENSTEAD RH	( )	100	62.0
08533	AA	BENTLEY P	( )	200	80.0
31098	A	BERNDT SJ	( )	675	78.2
37786	C	BERRY DG	( )	100	43.0
23172	B	BERRY DJ	( )	275	65.0
19647	A	BERRY K	( )	200	77.5
37652	C	BERRY M	( )	100	58.0
31924	A	BERRY PE	( )	400	74.7
00834	A	BEST P	( )	350	77.4
32605	B	BEST S	( )	100	63.0
21714	A	BESWICK WJ	( )	375	72.8
50972	C	BETHELL ST	( )	100	46.0
14389	B	BETTRIDGE R	( )	200	62.5
43948	B	BEVENS AR	( )	350	60.5
43949	C	BEVENS RB	( )	100	50.0
04915	A	BICKERS B G	( )	400	72.2
43554	B	BICKERTON D	( )	200	62.0
05719	AA	BIDWELL J	( )	500	87.6
44132	C	BIGGIN NIGEL J	( )	100	50.0
29382	C	BIGGIN RJ	( )	100	45.0
31149	B	BIGGINS JA	( )	200	67.0
22184	B	BIGGS J	( )	100	64.0
35980	B	BIGNELL DJ	( )	300	64.0

We might like to pretend that we can 'shoot a bit' but the inescapable truth comes through the post once a year in the shape of the official Averages Book.

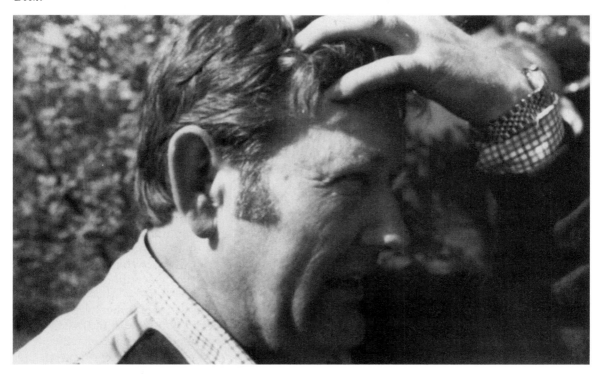

'How on earth did I miss that one?' Positive thinker Alan Secker, an English champion, relives the awful moment but is no doubt already hardening his resolve that whatever went wrong this time will not happen again.

149

win a class prize; as long as the targets are to his liking, the referee does not upset him and the background is ideal, this is bound to be his lucky day. It never is, of course. And the drive home does nothing to change things. His mind now is awash with the sort of recriminations that preyed on him on the way to the shooting ground. And the vicious circle will repeat itself next weekend, and the weekend after that, because he is not able to put set-backs into perspective and form a positive course of action to learn by his mistakes.

Positive thinking and, hence, positive action, can only start with a shooter being absolutely truthful with himself. This not only means identifying problem targets but also putting his finger on the things which on their own, or in combination, start that weekly slide into despair. We are mainly concerned here with our attitude as it relates to the positive side of shooting, not in trying to sort out those brought on by domestic strife or pressure of work. Marriage Guidance Counsellors and shooting do not mix so decide now which of the two is going to get your attention because you will never shoot to full potential if you go to the ground with a mind that is not on the job.

Let us stay with 'problem' targets a moment or two and look at ways of turning any feelings of self-doubt that might exist into positive action. If you miss every one that you fire at, it is plain that some form of help and advice is called for. What is needed here is a determination to find an instructor who can help iron out the difficulties. Pick up the telephone now and book a lesson. Do not leave it until next week, do it *now*. Delay, excuse-finding and not putting remedies into motion is the hallmark of a negative operator. Yet more often than not the solution to difficult targets lies in our own hands and big gains can be made by making ourselves understand how we hit the ones we did. Once we know how we broke six on that bogey stand of ours, we are well on the way to understanding why we missed the other four and

being able to use that knowledge to advantage next time out. What must be avoided at all costs is the feeling that six out of ten is not too bad and that, if we can get over half the targets, maybe next week we will enjoy a bit of luck and hit a few more.

Such thinking, of course, does not do anything to remove the seeds of anxiety which will surely surface when our gallant hoper meanders on to a similar stand at the following shoot only to miss the first pair out of the trap. He has got no idea why he missed them and suddenly all the doubts which have been smothered in 'if only' for the past seven days come flooding back and he makes a complete hash of the next four doubles.

In these situations it is all too easy to talk ourselves out of hitting targets because continued disappointment has a nasty habit of generating more and more self-doubt and gives negative thoughts a heaven-sent opportunity to take control. Worrying about targets only makes it doubly likely that you will miss them next time your paths cross as the vague mental pictures you have painted and stored are powerful enough to override the positive aspects of your technique. You need a crutch to help you through the next few difficult minutes but the one your brain produces is no use whatsoever because the images which fashioned it were crooked from the outset.

Positive thinking is not something which can be learnt in a classroom of like-minded students. It comes from within and is created, in the first place, by previous successes and the shooting technique that formed them. If inspiration is needed in times of crisis, a shooter must do what he can to cultivate a way of drawing on this resource and use it to full advantage. It is this ability, above all others, which helps to separate the man who regularly records a 90 per cent success rate from the 60 per cent man shooting alongside him, and makes his goals realistic and yours not.

Once you start to learn how to control your emotions and put what you know – rather than what you do not know – to work, progress will then be made. You might even

By all means check your score after each stand to make sure that the marker has not made any mistakes but do not dwell on your accumulating total – go on to each stand determined to break the lot.

151

If you find that you cannot shoot your way out of problems go back to your coach. Be honest with him and listen to what he has got to say.

Competition affects people in different ways. For some, concentration is a serious affair . . .

. . . while others respond to pressure by putting a brave face on it.

surprise yourself at how quickly improvements come about once the constraints have been lifted but do not be surprised if one or two hiccups do happen along the way – they are bound to. As far as your ability to break targets is concerned, any temporary set-back will probably be caused by over-confidence bypassing the technique that has done so well thus far and allowing bad habits to take over. If this is the case, things can quickly be put right again by paying renewed attention to detail when faced with targets which you have been starting to take for granted.

Always try to concentrate on what you are doing. This certainly does not mean staring hard at targets and keeping the brain cells working overtime between stands. Such activity can all too soon become counter-productive, tire the eyes and exhaust the mind. By all means watch targets closely and remain alert when you are on the firing line but do not overdo things. If you have got a long wait before it is your turn to shoot, have a chat with other shooters but avoid getting into a protracted conversation about the stand that you are about to tackle or the other targets you have still got to face. Other shooters' comments about what is in store can trigger off negative impulses so do not get too embroiled in the niceties of how much forward allowance these next few clays are going to need.

It does not always pay either to stand behind the safety cage watching each and every man in the queue shoot his allocation because this can induce a measure of boredom and over-familiarity with the targets. Instead, watch a couple of people go through the stand when you first get there and then leave it well alone until it is the turn of the shooter ahead of you. Use his targets to refresh your own memory and then get in there and shoot them.

A better way to describe concentration would be awareness: awareness of the way you shoot. In other words, when you are actually shooting you are not only paying attention to the target itself but also bringing into play your shooting technique as a way of fulfilling the image in your mind of what you are trying to achieve.

This is especially important if the birds you are about to shoot are a tough proposition. From what you have already seen of the targets, it can help to form a mental picture of your gun ahead of the clay, and the clay breaking when the trigger is squeezed. It might not work for everybody but it does help to keep anxiety at bay in a very positive manner. Anxiety, though, should not be confused with tension. From a positive thinker's viewpoint, anxiety is an admission of target uncertainty while tension is a by-product of success: the more he hits the higher it becomes – especially when he realises that not only is a good score in the offing but that it could be a winning one to boot. High tension can be a very destructive force indeed if a shooter allows it to swamp him or buckle his knees under the weight of what might be 'if only' he can shoot sixteen of the last twenty targets. In such situations tension quickly turns to anxiety. However, it can be a very potent ally, heightening concentration and releasing a flood of adrenalin that lets him storm through the rest of the field.

A sure sign that tension has turned to anxiety is when the tone, or pitch, of a shooter's voice changes when the target is called. Instead of being a confident 'Pull' it becomes a timid and muted sound or changes to a high-pitched squeak. Often the word 'Pull' is not discernible. All the referee and bystanders hear from the shooter is some sort of noise telling them he is ready and waiting for the next target to be let loose. Once this happens you can be fairly certain that he is feeling some turmoil and that if he does not take steps to get things back under control he is well on the way to missing one or more targets very soon.

When you are in a state of high tension or knee-trembling anxiety it is tempting to retrieve the situation by turning to the referee or crowd and exchanging a few light-hearted words. Some people take time aligning the letters on the cartridge heads before closing the gun in readiness for the next target; others might fish three or four shells out of their pocket and spend a few moments gazing at them while they decide which one to use – even though ·they are all the same brand!

There is no harm in this because it gives the shooter time to break the crushing pressure which otherwise might inexorably lead to a missed target. I would not recommend turning to the people behind for inspiration because it has a habit of breaking your chain of thought too completely – added to which is the very real possibility that some well-meaning wag might throw in a rib-tickling reply which sticks in the mind and leads to a very unfunny miss! If this ploy works for you, though, by all means stay with it. All shooters are different and the stimuli which work for one might well not work for another. When I sense that my voice is starting to reflect the state of the inner mind, or when I am unnecessarily rushing on to the next target, I find that the surest way of calming down is to take several deep breaths. Fill the lungs with air, hold it a moment or two and then expel all of it before taking in another deep draught. When you feel calmer and ready to take the next target, deflate the lungs and then take in a short gulp of air and give a short, confident call of 'Pull!' Do not overdo it by letting out a great big loud yell or hang on to the word as you see the target and start mounting the gun because the sound of your own voice will prove highly distracting.

It is worth bearing in mind, too, that a shooter's physical well-being on the day of the shoot can have an effect on his mental state. This is particularly so where food and drink are concerned. Mental application burns up calories, so during a long day's shooting it might become necessary to take a meal to prevent your senses becoming dulled. If you are used to chewing your way through a large luncheon each day then there is little point changing your routine and going without just for the sake of it. However, too much can be just as bad as too little and slow your

reactions down so be careful not to over-indulge. I feel that the wisest course (and it is a regime I stick to) is to have a good, solid, breakfast a couple of hours before the shoot. Not only will the meal keep you going most of the day but, by giving it a chance to get settled before shooting starts, you will not feel uncomfortably full either.

If you should start to feel peckish later in the day, rather than break off for lunch it is better to have a light snack. It will help supplement the body's own blood sugar levels and so keep you sharp and aware. A bar of chocolate sometimes helps too but do not be fooled by claims that its high sugar content gives your body's insulin levels a long-lasting boost – these claims are false. What it will do is create a fairly rapid peak but once your metabolism has burnt off this enriched supply the system can crash. The obvious answer here is to feed in another sugar-rich bar, but do not overdo it. Too much chocolate can have the opposite effect and actually slow you down. If you are concerned about keeping energy levels reasonably high the best course of action would be to carry a packet of glucose tablets and take one from time to time.

Do not make the mistake of going without fluids during the day either. Alcohol is definitely out until you have finished shooting for the day and it is not always a good idea to immerse the system in too much tea and coffee because of the caffeine content. This might well be a stimulant and keep you awake but the sheer volume intake can cause other problems – like where to find a toilet when you are surrounded by other shooters half a mile from the club-house! Again, when it comes to fluids, it is a case of being sensible and drinking only small quantities when you feel thirsty. Having said this, do not make the mistake of drinking too little if the weather turns warm because you run a high risk of dehydrating. It is unlikely that you will collapse or go dizzy but there is quite a likelihood that you could develop a distracting headache along with a debilitating lethargy.

By all means watch the targets but do not tire yourself out shooting everybody else's birds before stepping up to shoot your own.

Shooters are a funny bunch when talk comes down to undertaking a course of physical exercise as a means of keeping mind and body sharp. A lot tend to dismiss it as being both unnecessary and not a little strange. While I admit that I cannot see much point in embarking on a regime which involves punishing routines, I do go along with a programme aimed at improving stamina.

I like to think that my work on the shooting ground keeps me pretty active anyway but during the main competition season I like to top this up with a four mile run two or three times a week. The exercise helps pump a bit more oxygen into the bloodstream but, more important, it makes me feel sharper and able to maintain interest in whatever I am doing. It is probably psychological, but I do feel that this gentle exercise helps when it comes to a long day's shooting and, more especially, the three- or four-day competitions that set 200-bird FITASC Sporting championships apart from the rest.

To sum up then, mental agility in clay shooting boils down to little more than feeling good and having the confidence to put your trust in technique. Even the best shots suffer bad days so we can all draw some comfort from the fact that we are not alone in feeling low when things have gone wrong. The important thing is not to dwell on these setbacks; learn by the mistakes, identify where things went wrong but always look at the positive side of your shooting. It is the foundation on which your future shooting career will be built. May it be a long and happy one!

Index